Melissa Simson

DIABETIC
AIR FRYER
COOKBOOK

Low Sugar, Low Salt, Low Fat, Healthy Friendly
Air Fryer Recipes And a 30 Days Balanced Meal
Plan to Find a New, Salutary Lifestyle

Copyright - 2021 -Melissa Simson

All rights reserved.

The content contained within this book may not be reproduced, duplicated or transmitted without direct written permission from the author or the publisher.

Under no circumstances will any blame or legal responsibility be held against the publisher, or author, for any damages, reparation, or monetary loss due to the information contained within this book. Either directly or indirectly.

Legal Notice:

This book is copyright protected. This book is only for personal use. You cannot amend, distribute, sell, use, quote or paraphrase any part, or the content within this book, without the consent of the author or publisher.

Disclaimer Notice:

Please note the information contained within this document is for educational and entertainment purposes only. All effort has been executed to present accurate, up to date, and reliable, complete information. No warranties of any kind are declared or implied. Readers acknowledge that the author is not engaging in the rendering of legal, financial, medical or professional advice. The content within this book has been derived from various sources. Please consult a licensed professional before attempting any techniques outlined in this book.

By reading this document, the reader agrees that under no circumstances is the author responsible for any losses, direct or indirect, which are incurred as a result of the use of information contained within this document, including, but not limited to, - errors, omissions, or inaccuracies.

TABLE OF CONTENTS

INTRODUCTION	7
CHAPTER 1 - DIABETES & OBESITY	9
How Glucose & Insulin Work Together	9
Types of Diabetes	10
The Causes of Diabetes	11
Early Signs of Diabetes	12
CHAPTER 2 - HEALTHY LIVING & AIR-FRYING	15
How Works an Air Fryer	15
Cooking in an Air Fryer?	16
Tips for Cooking in an Air Fryer for Beginners	16
Benefits of Using Air Fryer	17
Healthy Living & Healthy Eating Habits	18
CHAPTER 3 - DIABETIC AIR FRYER BREAKFAST RECIPES	21
1. Asparagus Cheese Strata	22
2. Vegetable Frittata	23
3. Egg and Avocado Breakfast Burrito	24
4. Mixed Berry Dutch Pancake	25
5. Crunchy Fried French Toast Sticks	26
6. Pumpkin Oatmeal with Raisins	27
7. Mushroom and Black Bean Burrito	28
8. Bacon and Egg Sandwiches	29
9. Juicy Lamb Chops	30
10. Spicy Chicken Meatballs	31
11. Chicken Wings with Curry	32
12. Stuffed Chicken	33
13. Mesquite Pork Chops	34
14. Ranch Pork Chops	35
15. Pork Chops with Peanut Sauce	36
16. Glazed Pork Shoulder	37
17. Pork Shoulder with Pineapple Sauce	38
18. Bacon Wrapped Pork Tenderloin	39
19. Pork Tenderloin with Bell Peppers	40
20. Pork Tenderloin with Bacon & Veggies	41
21. Pork Loin with Potatoes	42
22. Stuffed Bell Peppers	43
23. Almond Crunch Granola	44
24. Yogurt Raspberry Cake	45
25. Spinach and Tomato Egg Cup	46
26. Egg Muffins with Bell Pepper	47
27. Egg-in-a-Hole	48
28. Egg and Cheese Pockets	49
29. Huevos Rancheros	50
30. Jalapeno Potato Hash	51
31. Goat Cheese Mixed Mushrooms	52
CHAPTER 4 - DIABETIC AIR FRYER POULTRY RECIPES	53

32. Mustard-Crusted Sole	54
33. Almond Crusted Cod with Chips	55
34. Stevia Lemon Snapper with Fruit	56
35. Easy Tuna Wraps	57
36. Asian-Inspired Swordfish Steaks	58
37. Salmon with Fennel and Carrot	59
38. Ranch Tilapia fillets	60
39. Chilean Sea Bass with Green Olive Relish	61
40. Ginger and Green Onion Fish	62
41. Asian Sesame Cod	63
42. Roasted Shrimp and Veggies	64
43. Lemon Scallops with Asparagus	65
44. Fish Tacos	66
45. Spicy Cajun Shrimp	67
46. Garlic Parmesan Roasted Shrimp	68
47. Quick Shrimp Scampi	69
48. Pork Spare Ribs	70
49. BBQ Pork Ribs	71

CHAPTER 5 - DIABETIC AIR FRYER MEAT RECIPES 73

50. Roasted Vegetable and Chicken Salad	74
51. Chicken Satay	75
52. Chicken Fajitas with Avocados	76
53. Crispy Buttermilk Fried Chicken	77
54. Garlicky Chicken with Creamer Potatoes	78
55. Baked Chicken Cordon Bleu	79
56. Chicken Tenders and Vegetables	80
57. Greek Chicken Kebabs	81
58. Tandoori Chicken	82
59. Stevia Lemon Garlic Chicken	83
60. Baked Lemon Pepper Chicken Drumsticks	84
61. Balsamic Glazed Chicken	85
62. Harissa Roasted Cornish Game Hens	86
63. Stevia Mustard Turkey Breast	87
64. South Indian Pepper Chicken	88
65. Mini Turkey Meatloaves	89

CHAPTER 6 - DIABETIC AIR FRYER VEGETABLES AND SIDES 91

66. Eggplant Surprise	92
67. Carrots and Turnips	93
68. Shrimp and Asparagus	94
69. Instant Brussels Sprouts with Parmesan	95
70. Braised Fennel	96
71. Brussels Sprouts & Potatoes Dish	97
72. Beet and Orange Salad	98
73. Endives Dish	99
74. Roasted Potatoes	100
75. Cabbage Wedges	101
76. Buffalo Cauliflower Wings	102
77. Sweet Potato Cauliflower Patties	103
78. Okra	104
79. Creamed Spinach	105
80. Eggplant Parmesan	106
81. Cauliflower Rice	107
82. Brussels Sprouts	108
83. Green Beans	109
84. Asparagus Avocado Soup	110
85. Fried Peppers with Sriracha Mayo	111
86. Classic Fried Pickles	112
87. Fried Green Beans with Pecorino Romano	113

88. Spicy Roasted Potatoes — 114
89. Spicy Glazed Carrots — 115
90. Easy Sweet Potato Bake — 116
91. Avocado Fries with Roasted Garlic Mayonnaise — 117
92. Roasted Broccoli with Sesame Seeds — 118
93. Corn on the Cob with Herb Butter — 119
94. Rainbow Vegetable Fritters — 120
95. Cauliflower and Goat Cheese Croquettes — 121

CHAPTER 7 - DIABETIC AIR FRYER SEAFOOD — 123

96. Crab Cake — 124
97. Salmon — 125
98. Parmesan Shrimp — 126
99. Fish Sticks — 127
100. Shrimp with Lemon and Chile — 128
101. Tilapia — 129
102. Tomato Basil Scallops — 130
103. Shrimp Scampi — 131
104. Salmon Cakes — 132
105. Cilantro Lime Shrimps — 133

CHAPTER 8 - DIABETIC AIR FRYER DESSERTS — 135

106. Pancakes — 136
107. Zucchini Bread — 137
108. Blueberry Muffins — 138
109. Baked Eggs — 139
110. Bagels — 140
111. Cauliflower Hash Browns — 141
112. Chicken Sandwich — 142
113. Tofu Scramble — 143
114. Fried Egg — 144
115. Cheesecake Bites — 145
116. Coconut Pie — 146
117. Crustless Cheesecake — 147
118. Chocolate Cake — 148
119. Chocolate Brownies — 149
120. Spiced Apples — 150
121. Pumpkin Custard — 151
122. Peanut Butter Banana "Ice Cream" — 152
123. Fruity Coconut Energy Balls — 153
124. Mini Apple Oat Muffins — 154
125. Dark Chocolate Almond Yogurt Cups — 155
126. Chocolate Avocado Mousse — 156
127. Pumpkin Spice Snack Balls — 157
128. Strawberry Lime Pudding — 158
129. Cinnamon Toasted Almonds — 159
130. Grain-Free Berry Cobbler — 160
131. Whole-Wheat Pumpkin Muffins — 161
132. Homemade Muffins — 162
133. Chocolate and Nut Cake — 163
134. Stevia Walnut Roasted Pears — 164
135. Almond Pears — 165

CHAPTER 9 - 30 DAY MEAL PLAN — 167
CONCLUSION — 171

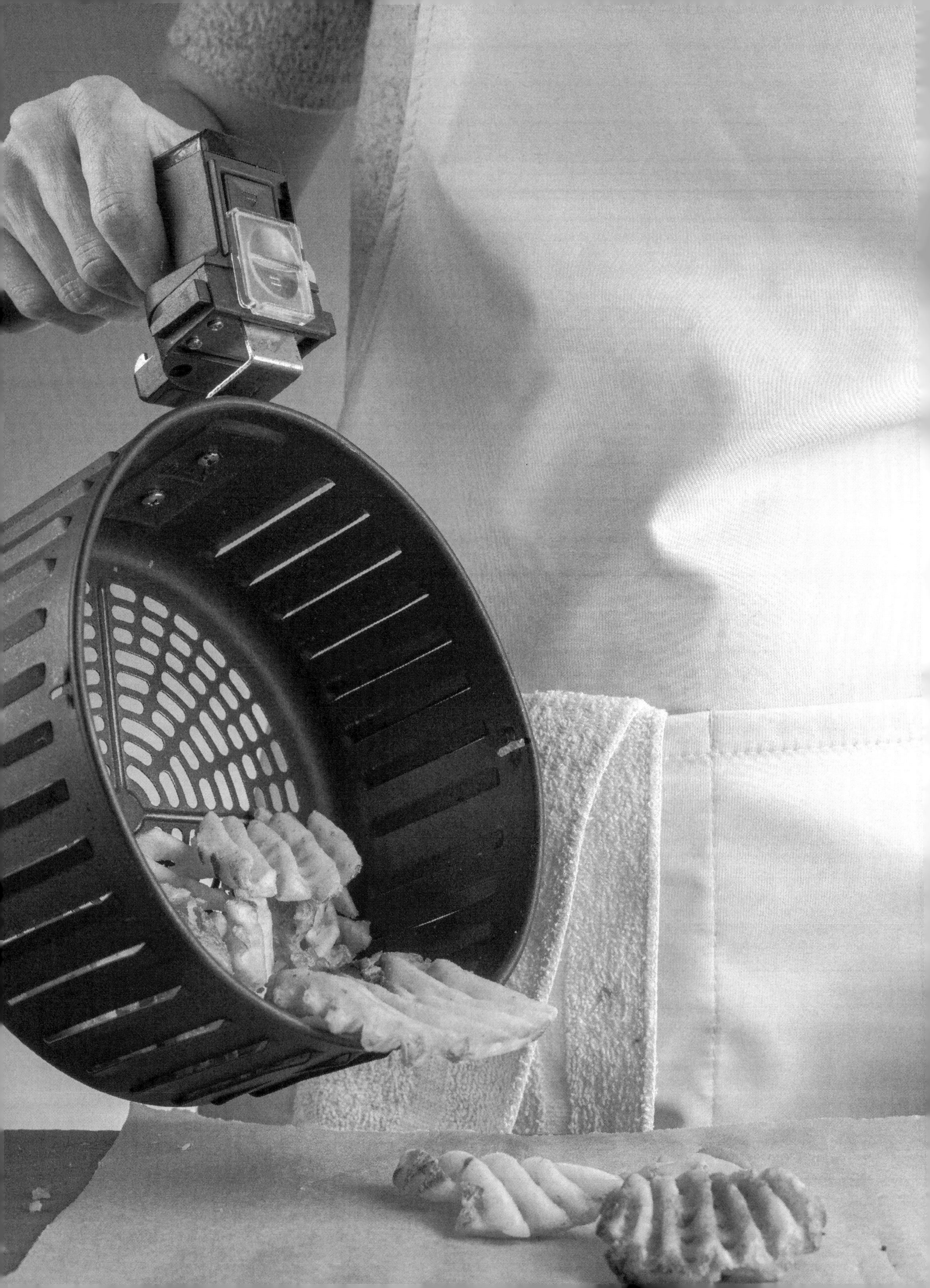

INTRODUCTION

Melissa Simson

Most of us know of someone in our circle of family or friends who lives with either type 1 or type 2 diabetes. Maybe we don't know who they are, and maybe that's because they don't talk to us about it. If we know who it is, maybe it's because we feel reluctant to ask them too many questions about their condition, because we are afraid to seem impolite. But, if we want to understand their condition, we really should ask them some questions. We should all become much more informed about the condition generally, so that we can help our friends and family members who have diabetes, to manage their healthcare regime and stay well. Besides, we should all take good care of our own general health through a sensible diet and regular exercise to help prevent the onset of type 2 diabetes, and other related health conditionsas we get older. It's just common sense.

Statistics are often seen as a boring subject, and people don't want to pay too much attention to them, but these recent figures from the World Health Organization are some that we should all look at closely. You might actually find them a little alarming.

Studies in 2014 showed that the number of people who have diabetes rose from 108 million in 1980 to 422 million in 2014. By 2014, more than 8.5% of adults aged 18 years and older had diabetes across the globe. That's one person in every eight! By the year 2016, diabetes was the direct cause of 1.6 million deaths worldwide. Even more alarmingly, the global prevalence of diabetes among adults over 18 years of age rose from 4.7% in 1980 to 8.5% in 2014. Almost double the numbers! Things have not improved: between 2000 and 2016, there was a 5% increase in premature mortality from diabetes. And it is not just the "developing" countries that swell the figures. In both high-income and low-income countries around the world, the premature mortality rate, directly due to diabetes, increased significantly in the 6 years between 2010 and 2016. These are figures that we absolutely cannot afford to ignore, as governments or as individuals.

This easy-to-follow, recipe-packed cookbook will help you to guide yourself towards a lifestyle of healthier eating. If you are not diabetic, the recipes are simply a healthy and delicious way to take care of your blood sugarlevels and carb. Intake and prevent obesity. If you are diabetic, these recipes will enable you to live your life to the fullest and to really enjoy preparing tasty meals that are fun to cook. But before you begin to try out the recipes on your family and friends, you really do need to understand what the condition is all about. We will answer some simple questions for you to help get you started: What are the differences between types 1 and 2 diabetes? Why are lifestyle choices and changes, such as quitting smoking, not drinking too much alcohol too frequently, eating sensibly, and taking regular exercise so important?

Chapter 1
DIABETES & OBESITY

Diabetes is a stubborn condition that arises from two reasons: whether when the pancreas cannot produce insulin enough for the body's needs or whenever the insulin it provides may not be utilized properly by the body. Insulin is a blood sugar-regulating hormone. Hyperglycemia, or high blood sugar, is a typical result of uncontrolled diabetes, causing significant harm to the body's structures, especially blood vessels and nerves over time. Diabetes mellitus is a category of illnesses that influence how the body uses glucose. Glucose is essential to your well-being. The primary issue of diabetes varies based on the type of diabetes, and this can result in excessive sugar in the blood, no matter what kind of diabetes a person has. If there is too much sugar, it can lead to grave health issues. The insulin hormone transfers the sugar into the cells from the blood.

High levels of blood sugar may cause harm to your kidneys, eyes, organs, and nerves. To understand what the main reason for diabetes is, you should know what the normal route of glucose consumption in the body is.

HOW GLUCOSE & INSULIN WORK TOGETHER
The pancreas is an organ situated behind and below the stomach that produces Insulin. It is a hormone that regulates the level of sugar in the blood. Here is a step-by-step production in the bloodstream,

insulin comes from the pancreases.

- Then Insulin helps the sugar to go into the body cells.
- Insulin reduces the level of sugar in the blood.
- Now that the level of sugar drops in blood, it also causes the pancreas to secret less amount of Insulin.
- As blood sugar level drops in the body, it reduces insulin secretion from the pancreas.

TYPES OF DIABETES

Diabetes mellitus, known as diabetes, is a metabolic condition that causes high blood sugar levels. The hormone insulin transfers sugar from the cells in the blood to be processed or used for nutrition. In diabetes, the body does not contain sufficient insulin or does not utilize the insulin it generates efficiently. Your brains, lungs, kidneys, and other organs may be affected by uncontrolled elevated blood sugar levels from diabetes.

There are different types of diabetes:

TYPE 1 DIABETES

A deficiency of the immune system, or is an autoimmune disease, results in type 1 diabetes, also called insulin-dependent diabetes or juvenile diabetes. In the pancreas, your immune system destroys the insulin-producing cells, killing the body's capacity to create insulin. It's not clear what causes autoimmune disease and how to treat it effectively. You have to take insulin to survive with type 1 diabetes. As an infant or young adult, several individuals are diagnosed. Only 10% of people with diabetes have type 1 diabetes. Symptoms that the body shows on the onset of type 1 diabetes are polyuria (excessive excretion of urine), polydipsia (extreme thirst), sudden weight loss, constant hunger, fatigue, and vision changes. These changes can occur suddenly.

TYPE 2 DIABETES

Type 2 diabetes, previously referred to as adult-onset diabetes or non-insulin-dependent, stems from insufficient insulin utilization by the body. Type 2 diabetes is found in the majority of individuals with diabetes. The symptoms can be identical to those with type 1 diabetes; however, much less marked, and as a consequence, when symptoms have already occurred, the condition can be detected after many years of diagnosis.

Type 2 diabetes happens when sugar starts adding up in your blood, and the body becomes resistant to insulin. Type 2 diabetes is insulin resistance, which ultimately leads to obesity. Obesity in itself is a collection of different diseases. Older generations were more susceptible, but younger generations are now being affected. This is a product of bad health, not enough nutrition, and fitness patterns. Your pancreas avoids utilizing insulin properly in type 2 diabetes. This creates complications with sugar that has to be taken out of the blood and placing it for energy in the cells. Finally, this will add to the need for insulin treatment.

Earlier stages, such as prediabetes, can be controlled successfully through food, exercise, and dynamic blood sugar control. This will also avoid the overall progression of type 2 diabetes. It is possible to monitor diabetes. In certain situations, if sufficient adjustments to the diet are created; on the contrary, the body will go into remission.

GESTATIONAL DIABETES

Hyperglycemia with blood glucose levels over average but below those diabetes levels is diagnosed with gestational diabetes. Gestational diabetes is identified via prenatal tests, rather than by signs recorded—high blood sugar, which also occurs during gestation. Hormones produced by the placenta are insulin-blocking, which is the main cause of this type of diabetes. You can manage gestational diabetes much of the time by food and exercise. Usually, it gets resolved after delivery. During pregnancy, gestational diabetes will raise the risk of complications. It will also increase the likelihood that both mothers and infants may experience type 2 diabetes later in life.

THE CAUSES OF DIABETES

CAUSES OF TYPE 1 DIABETES

The main cause of type 1 diabetes is unknown. It's understood that the immune system targets and eradicates the cells (in the pancreas) that produce insulin. The immune system usually destroys viruses or infectious bacteria. This leaves little or no insulin for the human body. Sugar keeps building up in the bloodstream instead of being transferred into the cells.

This type of diabetes is believed to be triggered by a mixture of hereditary susceptibility and the environment's variables, but it is still uncertain precisely what those variables are. It is not assumed that weight is a variable in type 1 diabetes. Type1 develops as the pancreas' beta cells that produce insulin are targeted and killed by the body's immune system, the body's ability to combat infection. Scientists assume that type 1 diabetes is triggered by genetic makeup and environmental causes that could induce the condition.

CAUSES OF PREDIABETES AND TYPE 2 DIABETES

Your cells can become immune to insulin's effect in prediabetes, which can happen in type 2 diabetes, and the pancreas is not able to generate sufficient insulin to counteract this resistance.

Sugar starts building up in your bloodstream instead of going to your cells, where it's required for fuel. It is unclear why this arises, while hereditary and environmental influences are thought to play A role in type 2 diabetes progression. The advancement of type 2 diabetes is closely related to being overweight, although not everybody with type 2 is obese. Several variables, including dietary conditions and genetic makeup, are responsible for the most prevalent type of diabetes.

Here are a few factors:

Insulin Resistance

Type 2 diabetes commonly progresses with insulin resistance, a disease in which insulin is not handled well by the body, liver, and fat cells. As a consequence, to enable glucose to reach cells, the body requires more insulin. The pancreas initially generates more insulin to maintain the additional demand. The pancreas can't create enough insulin over time, and blood glucose levels increase.

Overweight, Physical Inactivity, & Obesity

When you are not regularly involved and are obese or overweight, you are much more prone to have type 2 diabetes. Often, excess weight induces insulin resistance, which is prominent in persons with type 2 diabetes. In which area of the body stores, fat counts a lot. Insulin tolerance, type 2 diabetes, and heart and blood artery dysfunction are attributed to excess belly fat.

Genes &Family History

A family history of diabetes in the family makes it more probable that gestational diabetes may occur in a mother, which means that genes play a part. In African Americans, Asians, American Indians, and Latinas, Hispanic, mutations can also justify why the disease happens more frequently.

Any genes can make you more susceptible to advance type 2 diabetes type 1 diabetes.

Genetic makeup can make a person more obese, which in turn leads to having type 2 diabetes.

EARLY SIGNS OF DIABETES

Many of the same unmistakable warning signals are present with all forms of diabetes.

ITCHY SKIN & DRY MOUTH

Since the body requires water to urinate, most items provide less moisture. You can get dehydrated, and that might make your mouth taste dry, and dehydration also makes skin dry, which in result makes you itchy.

TIREDNESS & HUNGER

Your body transforms the food you consume intoglucose (sugar) that body cells use for fuel. But insulin is required by your cells to take in glucose, and if the body does not produce enough or none of the insulin, or if the insulin body produces is immune to your cells, the glucose can't get into them, and you don't have energy. This will leave you hungrier than normal and more drained.

URINATING & GETTING THIRSTIER

Normally, the typical person needs to pee four to seven times in one day, although developing diabetes may go a lot faster. Usually, when it moves into your liver, your body reabsorbs glucose. But as diabetes drives your blood sugar up, it may not be practical for your kidneys to get it all backdown. This allows more urine to be created by the liver, and it requires fluids. The outcome: you're going to have to urinate more frequently. You will get thirsty when you urinate too much, hence drinking more water.

BLURRED VISION

Your body cannot process fluids more efficiently, which leads to the swelling of lenses in your eyes. Hence, they have changed shape and cannot focus as before. It results in blurred vision.

Hence, to prevent the onset of diabetes it is important to eat healthily, stay active, eat less junk food, and more importantly, monitor your blood glucose levels regularly.

Chapter 2
HEALTHY LIVING & AIR-FRYING

An air fryer is comparable to the oven in the way that it roasts and bakes. Still, the distinction is that the heating elements are situated only on top and supported by a strong, large fan, which results in very crisp food in no time. The air fryer utilizes spinning heated air to easily and uniformly cook food instead of using a pot of hot oil. In order to encourage the hot air to flow evenly around the meal, the meal is put in a metal basket (mesh) or a rack, producing the very same light golden, crispy crunch you get from frying in oil. It is easy-to-use air fryers, cook food faster than frying, and clean up quickly. You can prepare a selection of healthy foods such as fruits, beef, seafood, poultry, and more, in addition to making beneficial variants of your favorite fried foods such as chips, onion rings, or French fries.

HOW WORKS AN AIR FRYER

The air fryer is a convective heat oven with a revved-up countertop. Its small room enables cooking much quicker. A heating device and a fan are kept at the top of the device. Hot air flows through and around food put in a basket-type fryer. This fast circulation, just like deep frying, renders the food crisp. It's also super quick to clean up, and most systems include dishwasher-safe components.

COOKING IN AN AIR FRYER?

Air fryers are quick, and they're used to heat frozen foods or cook all kinds of fresh food such as poultry, salmon, other seafood, pork chops, and vegetables once you learn how it works. Since they are still so moist, most meats don't need additional oil.

- Season them with salt and your favorite herbs and spices.

- Be sure you adhere to dry seasonings; less moisture contributes to outcomes that are crispier.

- Wait for the last few minutes of cooking, whether you choose to baste the beef with any sauce or barbecue sauce.

- Lean meat cuts, or items containing minimal or no fat, need browning and crisping needs a spray of oil. Before frying, clean the pork chops, boneless chicken breasts, and spray with a touch of oil. Due to the higher smoke point, vegetable oil or canola oil is generally preferred, which ensures that it can survive an air fryer's extreme heat.

- Before air-fry, vegetables often need to be sprayed with oil. Sprinkle them with salt. Use less than you usually would use. The air-fried crispy bits carry a great deal of flavor. You will love fried baby potato halves, broccoli florets, and Brussels sprouts. They're so crisp. Everything tends to get sweeter with sweet potatoes, butternut squash, peppers, and green beans do not need long at all.

TIPS FOR COOKING IN AN AIR FRYER FOR BEGINNERS

- Shake the basket:make sure to open the fryer and move food around while they cook in the device's tray, compressing smaller foods such as French fries and chips. Toss them every 5 to 10 minutes for better performance.

- Do not overcrowd the basket:giving plenty of room to foods so that the air will efficiently circulate is what gets you crispy outcomes.

- Spray oil on the food:make sure the food doesn't cling to the bowl, gently brush foods with cooking spray.

- Keep the food dry:to prevent splattering and excessive smoke, make sure food is dry before frying (even if you marinate it). In the same way, be sure to remove the grease from the bottom of the machine regularly while preparing high-fat items such as chicken wings.

- Know other functions of air frying:the air fryer is not just for frying; it is also perfect for other healthier cooking methods, such as grilling, baking, and roasting.

Few Other Tips

- Cut the food into equally sized parts for uniform cooking.

- Distribute the food in one, thin, even layer in the air fryer basket. If crowded the basket, food can be less crispy.

- A tiny amount of oil would create the very same light golden, crispy crust from frying. Using cooking spray or an oil mister to apply a thin, even coating oil to the food.

- The air fryer is valuable for reheating foods, particularly with a crispy crust that you want.

BENEFITS OF USING AIR FRYER

- Easy cleanup.
- Low-fat meals.
- Less oil is needed.
- Hot air cooks food evenly.
- Weight loss.
- Reduced cancer risk.
- Diabetes management.
- Improved memory.
- Improved gut health.

According to this food pyramid, you must consume a large portion of healthy vegetables and whole-grain starches, a balanced amount of healthy fats, and proteins with small amounts of nuts and oils.

HEALTHY LIVING & HEALTHY EATING HABITS

To obtain optimal health benefits, it is necessary to use the right combination of numerous nutrients. Generally, a healthy diet includes food from the following classes of foods:

- Starchy foods such as potatoes, bread, pasta, and rice in smaller portions.
- Big portions of vegetables and fruits.
- Little amounts of dairy and milk foods.
- Protein foods include meat, fish, and eggs.
- Protein (non-dairy), including beans, nuts, pulses, and tofu.
- The fifth food section that you consume is fatty and sugary goods. Sugary and fatty things can, though, make up just a limited portion of what you consume.
- Must eat salmon, sardines, and pilchards.
- Must eat dark green vegetables like broccoli and kale.
- Foods enriched in calcium-such as fruit juices and soya goods.
- Vitamin D allows the body to digest calcium, so try to go outdoors to receive vitamin D from the sun, have enough vitamin D-containing items, such as fortified cereal, fatty fish in the diet.
- It's necessary, substitute saturated fat with polyunsaturated fat.
- Consume at least five vegetable and fruit portions a day.
- Consume a minimum of two portions of fish each week (ideally fatty fish).
- Start consuming entire grains and nuts daily.
- Keep the sum of salt to very little, like 6g a day.
- Restricted the consumption of alcohol.

Limit or avoid the following in diet:

- Commercially manufactured or processed meats or readymade foods that are high in trans fatty acids and salt.
- Refined grains, such as dried cereals or white bread.
- Sweetened sugary beverages.
- High-calorie yet nutritionally weak foods, such as cookies, desserts, and crisps.

A well-balanced diet includes all of the following:

- You need the stamina to be productive during the day.
- Nutrients you need to develop and restore help you remain balanced and powerful and help avoid diet-related diseases, such as diabetes and certain cancers.
- You may also help sustain a healthier weight by staying busy and consuming a healthy, nutritious diet.
- Deficiencies of some vital nutrients, such as vitamins C, A, B, and E, and selenium, zinc, and iron, can impair the immune system's parts.
- You will reduce the chances of developing type 2 diabetes, and better heart health and will make your teeth & bones by keeping a healthier weight and consuming a nutritious diet low in saturated fat and rich in fiber that is found in whole grains.
- Eating a balanced diet in the proper amounts, coupled with exercise, will also help you lose weight, lower cholesterol and blood pressure levels, and reduce the chances of type 2 diabetes.

Here is how your blood glucose level should look like:

Mg/DL	Fusting	After Eating	2-3 Hours after Eating
Normal	80-100	170-200	120-140
Impaired Glucose	101-125	190-230	140-160
Diabetic	126 +	220-230	200+

Chapter 3
DIABETIC AIR FRYER BREAKFAST
RECIPES

1. ASPARAGUS CHEESE STRATA

Preparation Time: 12'

Cooking Time: 17'

Serving: 4

Ingredients:

6 asparagus spears, cut into 2-inch pieces.
2 slices whole-wheat bread, cut into ½-inch cubes.
4 eggs.
3 tbsp. whole milk.
½ cup grated Havarti or Swiss cheese.
2 tbsp. chopped flat-leaf parsley.
Pinch salt.
Freshly ground black pepper, to taste.

Directions:

1. Place the asparagus spears and 1 tbsp. water in a baking pan and place in the air fryer basket. Bake at 330°F (166°C) for 3 to 5 minutes or until crisp and tender. Remove the asparagus from the pan and drain it. Spray the pan with nonstick cooking spray.
2. Arrange the bread cubes and asparagus into the pan and set them aside.
3. In a medium bowl, beat the eggs with the milk until combined. Add the cheese, parsley, salt, and pepper. Pour into the baking pan.
4. Bake for 11 to 14 minutes or until the eggs are set and the top starts to brown.

Nutrition:

Calories: 167.
Fat: 9 g.
Protein: 12 g.
Carbs: 9 g.
Fiber: 2 g.
Sugar: 1 g.
Sodium: 200 mg.

2. VEGETABLE FRITTATA

Preparation Time:
10'

Cooking Time:
8-12'

Serving:
4

Directions:

1. In a baking pan, stir together the red bell pepper, onion, carrot, and olive oil. Put the pan into the air fryer. Bake at 350°F (177°C) for 4 to 6 minutes, shaking the basket once, until the vegetables are tender.
2. Meanwhile, in a medium bowl, beat the egg whites, egg, and milk until combined.
3. Pour the egg mixture over the vegetables in the pan. Sprinkle with the Parmesan cheese. Return the pan to the air fryer.
4. Bake for 4 to 6 minutes more, or until the frittata is puffy and set.
5. Cut into 4 wedges and serve.

Ingredients:

½ cup chopped red bell pepper.
⅓ cup minced onion.
⅓ cup grated carrot.
1 tsp. olive oil.
6 egg whites.
1 egg.
⅓ cup 2% milk.
1 tbsp. grated Parmesan cheese.

Nutrition:

Calories: 78.
Fat: 3 g.
Protein: 8 g.
Carbs: 5 g.
Fiber: 1 g.
Sugar: 3 g.
Sodium: 116 mg.

3. EGG AND AVOCADO BREAKFAST BURRITO

Preparation Time:
10'

Cooking Time:
3-5'

Serving:
4

Ingredients:

2 hard-boiled egg whites, chopped.
1 hard-boiled egg, chopped.
1 avocado, peeled, pitted, and chopped.
1 red bell pepper, chopped.
3 tbsp. low-sodium salsa, plus additional for serving (optional).
1 (1.2-oz./34-g) slice low-sodium, low-fat American cheese, torn into pieces.
4 low-sodium whole-wheat flour tortillas.

Directions:

1. In a medium bowl, thoroughly mix the egg whites, egg, avocado, red bell pepper, salsa, and cheese.
2. Place the tortillas on a work surface and evenly divide the filling among them. Fold in the edges and roll up. Secure the burritos with toothpicks if necessary.
3. Put the burritos in the air fryer basket. Air fry at 390°F (199°C) for 3 to 5 minutes, or until the burritos are light golden brown and crisp. Serve with more salsa (if using).

Nutrition:

Calories: 205.
Fat: 8 g.
Protein: 9 g.
Carbs: 27 g.
Fiber: 3 g.
Sugar: 1 g.
Sodium: 109 mg.

4. MIXED BERRY DUTCH PANCAKE

Preparation Time: 10'

Cooking Time: 12-16'

Serving: 4

Directions:

1. In a medium bowl, use an eggbeater or hand mixer to quickly mix the egg whites, egg, pastry flour, milk, and vanilla until well combined.
2. Use a pastry brush to grease the bottom of a baking pan with the melted butter. Immediately pour in the batter and put the baking pan in the fryer. Bake at 330°F (166°C) for 12 to 16 minutes, or until the pancake is puffed and golden brown.
3. Remove the pan from the air fryer; the pancake will fall. Top with strawberries, blueberries, and raspberries. Serve immediately.

Ingredients:

2 egg whites.
1 egg.
½ cup whole-wheat pastry flour.
½ cup 2% milk.
1 tsp. pure vanilla extract.
1 tbsp. unsalted butter, melted.
1 cup sliced fresh strawberries.
½ cup fresh blueberries.
½ cup fresh raspberries.

Nutrition:

Calories: 155.
Fat: 5 g.
Protein: 7 g.
Carbs: 21 g.
Fiber: 4 g.
Sugar: 6 g.
Sodium: 59 mg.

5. CRUNCHY FRIED FRENCH TOAST STICKS

Preparation Time:
6'

Cooking Time:
10-14'

Serving:
4

Ingredients:

3 slices low-sodium whole-wheat bread, each cut into 4 strips.
1 tbsp. unsalted butter, melted.
1 egg.
1 egg white.
1 tbsp. 2% milk.
1 tbsp. stevia.
1 cup sliced fresh strawberries.
1 tbsp. freshly squeezed lemon juice.

Directions:

1. Place the bread strips on a plate and drizzle with the melted butter.
2. In a shallow bowl, beat the egg, egg white, milk, and stevia.
3. Dip the bread into the egg mixture and place it on a wire rack to let the batter drip off.
4. Air fry half of the bread strips at 380°F (193°C) for 5 to 7 minutes, turning the strips with tongs once during cooking, until golden brown. Repeat with the remaining strips.
5. In a small bowl, mash the strawberries and lemon juice with a fork or potato masher. Serve the strawberry sauce with the French toast sticks.

Nutrition:

Calories: 145.
Fat: 5 g.
Protein: 7 g.
Carbs: 18 g.
Fiber: 3 g.
Sugar: 7 g.
Sodium: 120 mg.

6. PUMPKIN OATMEAL WITH RAISINS

Preparation Time:
10'

Cooking Time:
10'

Serving:
3 cups

Directions:

1. In a medium bowl, combine the rolled oats, raisins, ground cinnamon, and kosher salt, then stir in the pumpkin purée, maple syrup, and low-fat milk.
2. Spray a baking pan with nonstick cooking spray, then pour the oatmeal mixture into the pan and bake at 300°F (149°C) for 10 minutes.
3. Remove the oatmeal from the fryer and allow to cool in the pan on a wire rack for 5 minutes before serving.

Ingredients:

1 cup rolled oats.
2 tbsp. raisins.
¼ tsp. ground cinnamon.
Pinch of kosher salt.
¼ cup pumpkin purée.
2 tbsp. pure maple syrup.
1 cup low-fat milk.

Nutrition:

Calories: 304.
Fat: 4 g.
Protein: 10 g.
Carbs: 57 g.
Fiber: 6 g.
Sugar: 26 g.
Sodium: 140 mg.

7. MUSHROOM AND BLACK BEAN BURRITO

Preparation Time: 10'

Cooking Time: 15'

Serving: 1

Ingredients:

2 tbsp. canned black beans, rinsed and drained.
¼ cup sliced baby portobello mushrooms.
1 tsp. olive oil.
Pinch of kosher salt.
1 large egg.
1 slice low-fat Cheddar cheese.
1 (8-inch) whole-grain flour tortilla.
Hot sauce (optional).

Directions:

1. Spray a baking pan with nonstick cooking spray, then place the black beans and baby portobello mushrooms in the pan, drizzle with the olive oil, and season with the kosher salt.
2. Bake at 360°F (182°C) for 5 minutes, then pause the fryer to crack the egg on top of the beans and mushrooms. Bake for 8 more minutes or until the egg is cooked as desired.
3. Pause the fryer again, top the egg with cheese, and bake for 1 more minute.
4. Remove the pan from the fryer, then use a spatula to place the bean mixture on the whole-grain flour tortilla. Fold in the sides and roll from front to back. Serve warm with the hot sauce on the side (if using).

Nutrition:

Calories: 276.
Fat: 12 g.
Protein: 16 g.
Carbs: 26 g.
Fiber: 6 g.
Sugar: 2 g.
Sodium: 306 mg.

8. BACON AND EGG SANDWICHES

Preparation Time:
3'

Cooking Time:
8'

Serving:
2 sandwiches

Directions:

1. Spray two 3-inch ramekins with nonstick cooking spray, then crack one egg into each ramekin and add half the kosher salt and half the black pepper to each egg.
2. Place the ramekins in the fryer basket and bake at 360°F (182°C) for 5 minutes.
3. Pause the fryer and top each partially cooked egg with a slice of Canadian bacon and a slice of American cheese.
4. Bake for 3 more minutes or until the cheese has melted and the egg yolk has just cooked through.
5. Remove the ramekins from the fryer and allow to cool on a wire rack for 2 to 3 minutes, then flip the eggs, bacon, and cheese out onto English muffins and sprinkle some black pepper on top before serving.

Ingredients:

2 large eggs.
¼ tsp. kosher salt, divided.
¼ tsp. freshly ground black pepper, divided (plus extra for serving).
2 slices Canadian bacon.
2 slices American cheese.
2 whole-grain English muffins, sliced in half.

Nutrition:

Calories: 309.
Fat: 13 g.
Protein: 22 g.
Carbs: 26 g.
Fiber: 3g.
Sugar: 3g.
Sodium: 618mg.

9. JUICY LAMB CHOPS

Preparation Time: 14'

Cooking Time: 14'

Serving: 4

Ingredients:

4 lamb chops.
2 garlic cloves, minced.
2 tbsp. of olive oil.
Pepper.
Salt.

Directions:

1. Coat lamb chops with oil and rubs with garlic, pepper, and salt.
2. Place the dehydrating tray in a multi-level Air Fryer basket and place the basket in the instant pot.
3. Place lamb chops on dehydrating tray.
4. Seal pot with Air Fryer lid and select air fry mode then set the temperature to 350° F and timer for 14 minutes. Turn lamb chops halfway through.
5. Serve and enjoy.

Nutrition:

Calories: 313.
Fat: 16.9 g.
Carbs: 0.5 g.
Sugar: 0 g.
Protein: 38 g.
Cholesterol: 122 mg.

10. SPICY CHICKEN MEATBALLS

Preparation Time:
10'

Cooking Time:
11-14'

Serving:
24

Directions:

1. In a 6-by-2-inch pan, combine the red onion, garlic, jalapeño, and olive oil. Bake for 3 to 4 minutes in the Air Fryer, or until the vegetables are crisp-tender. Transfer to a medium bowl.
2. Mix in the almonds, egg, and thyme to the vegetable mixture. Add the chicken and mix until just combined.
3. Form the chicken mixture into about 24 (1-inch) balls. Bake the meatballs, in batches, for 8 to 10 minutes, until the chicken reaches an internal temperature of 165°F on a meat thermometer.

Ingredients:

1 medium red onion, minced.
2 garlic cloves, minced.
1 jalapeño pepper, minced.
2 tsp. of olive oil.
3 tbsp. of ground almonds.
1 egg.
1 tsp. of dried thyme.
1 pound of ground chicken breast.

Nutrition:

Calories: 185.
Fat: 7g (34% of calories from fat).
Saturated fat: 1g.
Protein: 29g.
Carbs: 5g.
Sodium: 55mg.
Fiber: 1g.
Sugar: 3g.
DV vitamin A: 2%
DV vitamin C: 10%

11. CHICKEN WINGS WITH CURRY

Preparation Time: 15'

Cooking Time: 20'

Serving: 4

Ingredients:

400 g chicken wings.
30 g curry.
1 tsp. of chili.
1 tsp. of cayenne pepper.
1 tsp. of salt.
1 lemon.
1 tsp. of basil.
1 tsp. of oregano.
3 tsp. of mustard.
1 tsp. of olive oil.

Directions:

1. Rub the wings with chili, curry, cayenne pepper, salt, basil, and oregano.
2. Put it in the bowl and mix it very carefully.
3. Leave the mixture at least for 10 minutes in the fridge.
4. Remove the mixture from the fridge and add mustard and sprinkle with chopped lemon. Stir the mixture gently again.
5. Spray the pan with olive oil and put the wings in it.
6. Preheat the Air Fryer oven to 180 °C and put wings there.
7. Cook it for 20 minutes.

Nutrition:

Calories: 244.
Proteins: 30.8 g.
Fats: 10.6 g.
Carbs: 7.2 g.

12. STUFFED CHICKEN

Preparation Time: 15'

Cooking Time: 30'

Serving: 4

Directions:

1. Make a "pocket" from the chicken breasts and rub it with black pepper and cayenne pepper.
2. Slice tomatoes and chop basil.
3. Chop the goat cheese.
4. Combine all the ingredients together—it will be the filling for breasts.
5. Fill the chicken breasts with this mixture.
6. Take a needle, thread, and sew "pockets."
7. Preheat the Air Fryer oven to 200°C. Place the chicken breasts in the tray and pour it with tomato juice.
8. Serve.

Ingredients:

2 chicken breasts.
2 tomatoes.
200 g basil.
1 tsp. of black pepper.
1 tsp. of cayenne pepper.
100 g of tomato juice.
40 g of goat cheese.

Nutrition:

Calories: 312.
Proteins: 41.6 g.
Fats: 13.4 g.
Carbs: 5.6 g.

13. MESQUITE PORK CHOPS

Preparation Time: 10'

Cooking Time: 14'

Serving: 2

Ingredients:

2 pork chops.
1 tbsp. of olive oil.
2 tbsp. of stevia.
1 1/2 tbsp. of mesquite seasoning pepper.
Salt.

Directions:

1. Mix together oil, stevia, mesquite seasoning, pepper, salt and rub all over pork chops.
2. Place the dehydrating tray in a multi-level Air Fryer basket and place the basket in the instant pot.
3. Place pork chops on dehydrating tray.
4. Seal pot with Air Fryer lid and select air fry mode, then set the temperature to 380 °F and timer for 14 minutes. Turn pork chops halfway through.
5. Serve and enjoy.

Nutrition:

Calories: 390.
Fat: 27.1 g.
Carbs: 19.1 g.
Sugar: 17.3 g.
Protein: 18.4 g.
Cholesterol: 69 mg.

14. RANCH PORK CHOPS

Preparation Time:
10'

Cooking Time:
12'

Serving:
4

Directions:

1. In a shallow bowl, whisk egg, milk, pepper, and salt.
2. In a shallow dish, mix together breadcrumbs and ranch seasoning.
3. Dip pork chops in egg and coat with breadcrumbs.
4. Place the dehydrating tray in a multi-level Air Fryer basket and place the basket in the instant pot.
5. Place pork chops on dehydrating tray.
6. Seal pot with Air Fryer lid and select air fry mode then set the temperature to 360 ºF and timer for 12 minutes. Turn pork chops halfway through.
7. Serve and enjoy.

Ingredients:

4 pork chops.
1 egg, lightly beaten.
1 packet of ranch seasoning.
2 cups breadcrumbs.
1/2 cup of milk.
Pepper.
Salt.

Nutrition:

Calories: 522.
Fat: 24.5 g.
Carbs: 40.5 g.
Sugar: 4.8 g.
Protein: 27.6 g.
Cholesterol: 112 mg.

15. PORK CHOPS WITH PEANUT SAUCE

Preparation Time: 20'

Cooking Time: 12'

Serving: 4

Ingredients:

For chops:
1 tsp. of fresh ginger, minced.
1 garlic clove, minced.
2 tbsp. of soy sauce.
1 tbsp. of olive oil.
1 tsp. of hot pepper sauce.
1-pound of boneless pork chop, cubed into 1-inch size.

For peanut sauce:
1 tbsp. of olive oil.
1 shallot, finely chopped.
1 garlic clove, minced.
1 tsp. of ground coriander.
¾ cup of ground peanuts.
1 tsp. of hot pepper sauce.
¾ cup of coconut milk.

Directions:

1. For the pork: in a bowl, mix together the ginger, garlic, soy sauce, oil, and hot pepper sauce.
2. Add the pork chops and generously coat with mixture.
3. Place at room temperature for about 15 minutes.
4. Set the temperature of the Air Fryer to 390°F. Grease an Air Fryer basket.
5. Arrange chops into the prepared Air Fryer basket in a single layer.
6. Air fry for about 12 minutes.
7. Meanwhile, for the sauce: in a pan, heat oil over medium heat and sauté the shallot and garlic for about 2 to 3 minutes.
8. Add the coriander and sauté for about 1 minute.
9. Stir in the remaining ingredients and cook for about 5 minutes, stirring continuously.
10. Remove the pan of sauce from heat and let it cool slightly.
11. Remove the chops from Air Fryer and transfer onto serving plates.
12. Serve immediately with the topping of peanut sauce.

Nutrition:

Calories: 725.
Carbs: 9.5g.
Protein: 34.4g.
Fat: 62.9g.
Sugar: 2.8g.
Sodium: 543mg.

16. GLAZED PORK SHOULDER

Preparation Time:
15'

Cooking Time:
18'

Serving:
5

Directions:

1. In a bowl, mix together all the soy sauce, and stevia.
2. Add the pork and generously coat it with marinade.
3. Cover and refrigerate to marinate for about 4 to 6 hours.
4. Set the temperature of the Air Fryer to 335°F. Grease an Air Fryer basket.
5. Place the pork shoulder into the prepared Air Fryer basket.
6. Air fry for about 10 minutes and then, another 6 to 8 minutes at 390°F.
7. Remove from Air Fryer and transfer the pork shoulder onto a platter.
8. With a piece of foil, cover the pork for about 10 minutes before serving.
9. Enjoy!

Ingredients:

1/3 cup of soy sauce.
1 tbsp. of stevia.
2 pounds of pork shoulder, cut into 1½-inch thick slices.

Nutrition:

Calories: 475.
Carbs: 8g.
Protein: 36.1g.
Fat: 32.4g.
Sugar: 7.1g.
Sodium: 165mg.

17. PORK SHOULDER WITH PINEAPPLE SAUCE

Preparation Time: 20'

Cooking Time: 24'

Serving: 3

Ingredients:

For pork:
10½ oz. of pork shoulder, cut into bite-sized pieces.
2 pinches of Maggi seasoning.
1 tsp. of light soy sauce.
Dash of sesame oil.
1 egg.
¼ cup of plain flour.

For sauce:
1 tsp. of olive oil.
1 medium of onion, sliced.
1 tbsp. of garlic, minced.
1 large pineapple slice, cubed.
1 medium tomato, chopped.
2 tbsp. of tomato sauce.
2 tbsp. of oyster sauce.
1 tbsp. of Worcestershire sauce.
1 tbsp. of water.
½ tbsp. of corn flour.

Nutrition:

Calories: 557.
Carbs: 57.5g.
Protein: 28.8g.
Fat: 25.1g.
Sugar: 35.1g.
Sodium: 544mg.

Directions:

1. For the pork: in a large bowl, mix together the Maggi seasoning, soy sauce, and sesame oil.
2. Add the pork cubes and generously mix them with the mixture.
3. Refrigerate to marinate for about 4 to 6 hours.
4. In a shallow dish, beat the egg.
5. In another dish, place the plain flour.
6. Dip the cubed pork in 1 beaten egg and then, coat evenly with the flour.
7. Set the temperature of the Air Fryer to 248°F. Grease an Air Fryer basket.
8. Arrange pork cubes into the prepared Air Fryer basket in a single layer.
9. Air fry for about 20 minutes.
10. Meanwhile, for the sauce: in a skillet, heat oil over medium heat and sauté the onion and garlic for about 1 minute.
11. Add the pineapple and tomato and cook for about 1 minute.
12. Add the tomato sauce, oyster sauce, Worcestershire sauce, and stir to combine.
13. Meanwhile, in a bowl, mix together the water and the corn flour.
14. Add the corn flour mixture into the sauce, stirring continuously.
15. Cook until the sauce is thickened enough, stirring continuously.
16. Remove pork cubes from Air Fryer and add them into the sauce.
17. Cook for about 1 to 2 minutes or until coated completely.
18. Remove from the heat and serve hot.

NOTE: if you don't have fresh pineapple in your hands, then you can use canned pineapple.

18. BACON WRAPPED PORK TENDERLOIN

Preparation Time: 15'

Cooking Time: 30'

Serving: 4

Directions:

1. Coat the tenderloin evenly with mustard.
2. Wrap the tenderloin with bacon strips.
3. Set the temperature of the Air Fryer to 360°F. Grease an Air Fryer basket.
4. Arrange pork tenderloin into the prepared Air Fryer basket.
5. Air fry for about 15 minutes.
6. Flip and air fry for another 10 to 15 minutes.
7. Remove from Air Fryer and transfer the pork tenderloin onto a platter, wait for about 5 minutes before slicing.
8. Cut the tenderloin into desired size slices and serve.

Ingredients:

1: 1½ pound of pork tenderloins.
4 bacon strips.
2 tbsp. of Dijon mustard.

Nutrition:

Calories: 504.
Carbs: 0.8g.
Protein: 61.9.
Fat: 26.2g.
Sugar: 9.1g.
Sodium: 867mg.

19. PORK TENDERLOIN WITH BELL PEPPERS

Preparation Time: 20'

Cooking Time: 15'

Serving: 3

Ingredients:

1 big red bell pepper, seeded and cut into thin strips.
1 red onion, thinly sliced.
2 tsp. of herbs de Provence.
Salt and ground black pepper, as required.
1 tbsp. of olive oil.
10½-oz. of pork tenderloin, cut into 4 pieces.
½ tbsp. of Dijon mustard.

Directions:

1. In a bowl, add the bell pepper, onion, herbs de Provence, salt, black pepper, and ½ tbsp. of oil and toss to coat well.
2. Rub the pork pieces with mustard, salt, and black pepper.
3. Drizzle with the remaining oil.
4. Set the temperature of the Air Fryer to 390°F. Grease an Air Fryer pan.
5. Place bell pepper mixture into the prepared Air Fryer pan and top with the pork pieces.
6. Air fry for about 15 minutes, flipping once halfway through.
7. Remove from Air Fryer and transfer the pork mixture onto serving plates.
8. Serve hot.

Nutrition:

Calories: 218.
Carbs: 7.1g.
Protein: 27.7g.
Fat: 8.8g.
Sugar: 3.7g.
Sodium: 110mg.

20. PORK TENDERLOIN WITH BACON & VEGGIES

Preparation Time:
20'

Cooking Time:
28'

Serving:
3

Directions:

1. Set the temperature of the Air Fryer to 390°F. Grease an Air Fryer basket.
2. With a fork, pierce the potatoes.
3. Place potatoes into the prepared Air Fryer basket and air fry for about 15 minutes.
4. Wrap one bacon slice around 4 to 6 green beans.
5. Coat the pork tenderloins with oil.
6. After 15 minutes, add the pork tenderloins into the Air Fryer basket with potatoes and air fry for about 5 to 6 minutes.
7. Remove the pork tenderloins from the basket.
8. Place bean rolls into the basket and top with the pork tenderloins.
9. Air fry for another 7 minutes.
10. Remove from the Air Fryer and transfer the pork tenderloins onto a platter.
11. Cut each tenderloin into desired size slices.
12. Serve alongside the potatoes and green beans rolls.

Ingredients:

3 potatoes.
¾ pound of frozen green beans.
6 bacon slices.
36-oz. of pork tenderloins.
2 tbsp. of olive oil.

Nutrition:

Calories: 918.
Carbs: 42.4 g.
Protein: 77.9g.
Fat: 47.7g.
Sugar: 4g.
Sodium: 1400mg.

21. PORK LOIN WITH POTATOES

Preparation Time: 15'

Cooking Time: 25'

Serving: 5'

Ingredients:

2 pounds of pork loin.
3 tbsp. of olive oil, divided.
1 tsp. of fresh parsley, chopped.
Salt and ground black pepper, as required.
3 large red potatoes, chopped.
½ tsp. of garlic powder.
½ tsp. of red pepper flakes, crushed.

Directions:

1. Coat the pork loin with oil and then season evenly with parsley, salt, and black pepper.
2. In an enormous bowl, mix the potatoes, remaining oil, garlic powder, red pepper flakes, salt, and black pepper and toss to coat well.
3. Set the temperature of the Air Fryer to 325°F. Grease an Air Fryer basket.
4. Place loin into the prepared Air Fryer basket.
5. Arrange potato pieces around the pork loin.
6. Air fry for about 25 minutes.
7. Remove from Air Fryer and transfer the pork loin onto a platter, wait for about 5 minutes before slicing.
8. Cut the pork loin into desired size slices and serve alongside the potatoes.

Nutrition:

Calories: 556.
Carbs: 29.6g.
Protein: 44.9g.
Fat: 28.3g.
Sugar: 1.9g.
Sodium: 132mg.

22. STUFFED BELL PEPPERS

Preparation Time:
10-20'

Cooking Time:
30'

Serving:
4

Directions:

1. In a bowl, mix sour cream with chipotle in adobo sauce, lime zest and lime juice and garlic powder, stir well and keep in the fridge until you serve it.
2. In a bowl, mix turkey meat with green onions, green chilies, breadcrumbs, jalapeno, cumin, salt, chili powder and garlic powder, stir very well and stuff your peppers with this mix.
3. Add 1 cup water to your instant pot, add peppers in the steamer basket, close the lid and cook at High for 15 minutes.
4. Release the pressure naturally for 10 minutes, then release the remaining pressure by turning the valve to 'Venting,' transfer bell peppers to a pan, add cheese on top, introduce in preheated broiler and broil until cheese is browned.
5. Divide bell peppers on plates, top with the chipotle sauce you've made earlier and serve.

Ingredients:

1 lb. of turkey meat, ground.
5 oz. of canned green chilies; chopped.
1 cup of water.
1 jalapeno pepper; chopped.
2 tsp. of chili powder.
1 tsp. of garlic powder.
1 tsp. of cumin, ground.
2 green onions; chopped.
1 avocado; chopped.
Salt to the taste.
1/2 cup of whole wheat panko.
4 bell peppers, tops, and seeds discarded.
4 pepper jack cheese slices.
Crushed tortilla chips.
Pico de Gallo.

For the chipotle sauce:
Zest from 1 lime.
Juice from 1 lime.
1/2 cup of sour cream.
2 tbsp. of chipotle in adobo sauce.
1/8 tsp. of garlic powder.

Nutrition:

Calories: 220.
Fat: 11g.
Protein: 5g.
Sugar: 2g.
Carbs: 13g.
Fiber: 4g.
Sodium: 325mg.
Cholesterol: 67mg.

23. ALMOND CRUNCH GRANOLA

Preparation Time: 5'

Cooking Time: 8-10'

Serving: 1/3 Cups

Ingredients:

⅔ cup rolled oats.
⅓ cup unsweetened shredded coconut.
⅓ cup sliced almonds.
1 tsp. canola oil.
2 tsp. stevia.
¼ tsp. kosher salt.

Directions:

1. In a medium bowl, combine the rolled oats, shredded coconut, sliced almonds, canola oil, stevia, and kosher salt.
2. Place a small piece of parchment paper on the bottom of a baking pan, then pour the mixture into the pan and distribute it evenly. Bake at 360°F (182°C) for 5 minutes, pause the fryer to gently stir the granola and bake for 3 more minutes.
3. Remove the granola from the fryer and allow to cool in the pan on a wire rack for 5 minutes, then transfer the granola to a serving plate to cool completely before serving. It becomes crunchier as it cools. Store the granola in an airtight container for up to 2 weeks.

Nutrition:

Calories: 181.
Fat: 9 g.
Protein: 4 g.
Carbs: 21 g.
Fiber: 5 g.
Sugar: 4 g.
Sodium: 94 mg.

24. YOGURT RASPBERRY CAKE

Preparation Time:
10'

Cooking Time:
8'

Serving:
4 Slices

Directions:

1. In a large bowl, combine the whole wheat pastry flour, kosher salt, and baking powder, then stir in the whole milk vanilla yogurt, canola oil, and maple syrup and gently fold in the raspberries.
2. Spray a baking pan with nonstick cooking spray, then pour the cake batter into the pan and bake at 300°F (149°C) for 8 minutes.
3. Remove the cake from the fryer and allow it to cool in the pan on a wire rack for 10 minutes before cutting and serving.

Ingredients:

½ cup whole wheat pastry flour.
⅛ tsp. kosher salt.
¼ tsp. baking powder.
½ cup whole milk vanilla yogurt.
2 tbsp. canola oil.
2 tbsp. pure maple syrup.
¾ cup fresh raspberries.

Nutrition:

Calories: 168.
Fat: 8g.
Protein: 3g.
Carbs: 21g.
Fiber: 3 g.
Sugar: 8g.
Sodium: 82mg.

25. SPINACH AND TOMATO EGG CUP

Preparation Time: 5'

Cooking Time: 10'

Serving: 1

Ingredients:

2 egg whites, beaten.
2 tbsp. chopped tomato.
2 tbsp. chopped spinach.
Pinch of kosher salt.
Red pepper flakes (optional).

Directions:

1. Spray a 3-inch ramekin with nonstick cooking spray, then combine the egg whites, tomato, spinach, kosher salt, and red pepper flakes (if using) in the ramekin.
2. Place the ramekin in the air fryer basket and bake at 300°F (149°C) for 10 minutes or until the eggs have set.
3. Remove the ramekin from the fryer and allow to cool on a wire rack for 5 minutes before serving.

Nutrition:

Calories: 32.
Fat: 0 g.
Protein: 7 g.
Carbs: 1 g.
Fiber: 1 g.
Sugar: 1 g.
Sodium: 184 mg.

26. EGG MUFFINS WITH BELL PEPPER

Preparation Time:
5'

Cooking Time:
10'

Serving:
2

Directions:

1. In a large bowl, whisk together the eggs, then stir in the bell pepper, red onion, kosher salt, and black pepper.
2. Spray two 3-inch ramekins with nonstick cooking spray, then pour half the egg mixture into each ramekin and place the ramekins in the fryer basket. Bake at 390°F (199°C) for 8 minutes.
3. Pause the fryer, sprinkle 1 tbsp. of shredded Cheddar cheese on top of each cup, and bake for 2 more minutes.
4. Remove the ramekins from the fryer and allow to cool on a wire rack for 5 minutes, then turn the omelet cups out on plates and sprinkle some black pepper on top before serving.

Ingredients:

4 large eggs.
½ bell pepper, finely chopped.
1 tbsp. finely chopped red onion.
¼ tsp. kosher salt.
¼ tsp. freshly ground black pepper, plus extra for serving.
2 tbsp. shredded Cheddar cheese.

Nutrition:

Calories: 172.
Fat: 12 g.
Protein: 14 g.
Carbs: 2 g.
Fiber: 0 g.
Sugar: 1 g.
Sodium: 333 mg.

27. EGG-IN-A-HOLE

Preparation Time: 5'

Cooking Time: 5-7'

Serving: 1

Ingredients:

1 slice whole-grain bread.
1 large egg.
⅛ tsp. kosher salt.
¼ cup diced avocado.
¼ cup diced tomato.
Pinch of freshly ground black pepper.

Directions:

1. Spray a baking pan with nonstick cooking spray, then use a ring mold or a sharp knife to cut a 3-inch hole in the center of the whole-grain bread. Place the bread slice and the circle in the pan.
2. Crack the egg into the hole, then season with the kosher salt. Bake at 360°F (182°C) for 5 to 7 minutes or until the egg is cooked as desired.
3. Remove the pan from the fryer and allow to cool on a wire rack for 5 minutes before transferring the toast to a plate, then sprinkle the avocado, tomato, and black pepper on top before serving.

Nutrition:

Calories: 220.
Fat: 12 g.
Protein: 10 g.
Carbs: 18 g.
Fiber: 5 g.
Sugar: 4 g.
Sodium: 406 mg.

28. EGG AND CHEESE POCKETS

Preparation Time: 10'

Cooking Time: 35'

Serving: 4 pockets

Directions:

1. Pour the egg into a baking pan, season with the kosher salt, and bake at 330°F (166°C) for 3 minutes. Pause the fryer, gently scramble the egg, and bake for 2 more minutes. Remove the egg from the fryer, keeping the fryer on, and set the egg aside to slightly cool.
2. Roll the puff pastry out flat and divide into 4 pieces.
3. Place a piece of Cheddar cheese and ¼ of the egg on one side of a piece of pastry, fold the pastry over the egg and cheese, and use a fork to press the edges closed. Repeat this process with the remaining pieces.
4. Place 2 pockets in the fryer and bake for 15 minutes or until golden brown. Repeat this process with the other 2 pockets.
5. Remove the pockets from the fryer and allow to cool on a wire rack for 5 minutes before serving.

Ingredients:

1 large egg, beaten.
Pinch of kosher salt.
½ sheet puff pastry.
1 slice Cheddar cheese, divided into 4 pieces.

Nutrition:

Calories: 215.
Fat: 15 g.
Protein: 6 g.
Carbs: 14 g.
Fiber: 0 g.
Sugar: 0 g.
Sodium: 143 mg.

29. HUEVOS RANCHEROS

Preparation Time: 20'

Cooking Time: 25'

Serving: 4

Ingredients:

4 large eggs.
¼ tsp. kosher salt.
¼ cup masa harina (corn flour).
1 tsp. olive oil.
¼ cup warm water.
½ cup salsa.
¼ cup crumbled queso fresco or feta cheese.

Directions:

1. Crack the eggs into a baking pan, season with the kosher salt, and bake at 330°F (166°C) for 3 minutes. Pause the fryer, gently scramble the eggs, and bake for 2 more minutes. Remove the eggs from the fryer, keeping the fryer on, and set the eggs aside to slightly cool. (Clean the baking pan before making the tortillas.)
2. Increase the temperature to 390°F (199°C).
3. In a medium bowl, combine the masa harina, olive oil, and ¼ tsp. of kosher salt by hand, then slowly pour in the water, stirring until a soft dough forms.
4. Divide the dough into 4 equal balls, then place each ball between 2 pieces of parchment paper and use a pie plate or a rolling pin to flatten the dough.
5. Spray the baking pan with nonstick cooking spray, then place one flattened tortilla in the pan and air fry for 5 minutes. Repeat this process with the remaining tortillas.
6. Remove the tortillas from the fryer and place them on a serving plate, then top each tortilla with the scrambled eggs, salsa, and cheese before serving.

Nutrition:

Calories: 136.
Fat: 8 g.
Protein: 8 g.
Carbs: 8 g.
Fiber: 1 g.
Sugar: 2 g.
Sodium: 333 mg.

30. JALAPENO POTATO HASH

Preparation Time: 10'

Cooking Time: 19-20'

Serving: 4 Cups

Directions:

1. Cook the sweet potatoes on high in the microwave until softened but not completely cooked (3 to 4 minutes), then set aside to cool for 10 minutes.
2. Remove the skins from the sweet potatoes, then cut the sweet potatoes into large chunks.
3. In a large bowl, combine the sweet potatoes, red onion, green bell pepper, jalapeño pepper, kosher salt, black pepper, and olive oil, tossing gently.
4. Spray the air fryer basket with nonstick cooking spray, then pour the mixture into the basket and air fry at 360°F (182°C) for 8 minutes.
5. Pause the fryer to shake the basket, then air fry for 8 more minutes or until golden brown.
6. Remove the hash from the fryer, place on a plate lined with a paper towel, and allow to cool for 5 minutes, then add the poached egg, sprinkle black pepper on top, and serve.

Ingredients:

2 large sweet potatoes.
½ small red onion, cut into large chunks.
1 green bell pepper, cut into large chunks.
1 jalapeño pepper, seeded and sliced.
½ tsp. kosher salt.
¼ tsp. freshly ground black pepper, plus extra for serving.
1 tsp. olive oil.
1 large egg, poached.

Nutrition:

Calories: 131.
Fat: 3g.
Protein: 4g.
Carbs: 22g.
Fiber: 4g.
Sugar: 7g.
Sodium: 174mg.

31. GOAT CHEESE MIXED MUSHROOMS

Preparation Time:
10'

Cooking Time:
10'

Serving:
4

Ingredients:

3 tbsp. vegetable oil.
1 pound (454 g) mixed mushrooms, trimmed and sliced.
1 clove garlic, minced.
¼ tsp. dried thyme.
½ tsp. black pepper.
4 oz. (113 g) goat cheese, diced.
2 tsp. chopped fresh thyme leaves (optional).

Directions:

1. In a baking pan, combine the oil, mushrooms, garlic, dried thyme, and pepper. Stir in the goat cheese. Place the pan in the air fryer basket. Roast at 400°F (204°C) for 10 minutes, stirring halfway through the cooking time.
2. Sprinkle with fresh thyme, if desired.

Nutrition:

Calories: 248.
Fat: 20 g.
Protein: 12 g.
Carbs: 5 g.
Fiber: 1 g.
Sugar: 2 g.
Sodium: 126 mg.

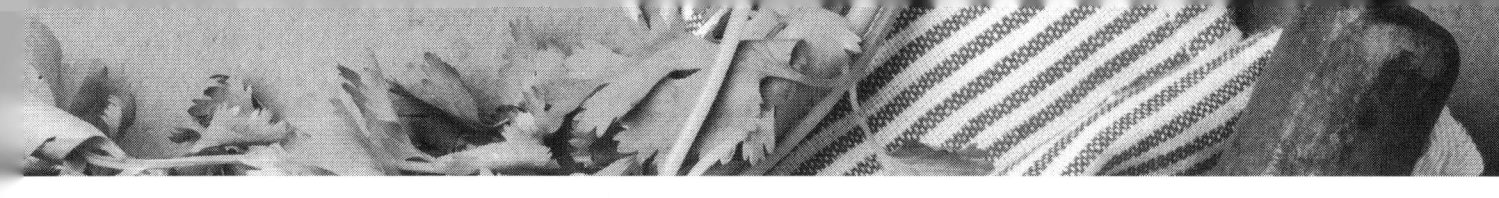

Chapter 4
DIABETIC AIR FRYER POULTRY
RECIPES

32. MUSTARD-CRUSTED SOLE

Preparation Time: 5'

Cooking Time: 8-11'

Serving: 4

Ingredients:

5 tsp. low-sodium yellow mustard.
1 tbsp. freshly squeezed lemon juice.
4 (3½-oz. / 99-g) sole fillets.
½ tsp. dried thyme.
½ tsp. dried marjoram.
⅛ tsp. freshly ground black pepper.
1 slice low-sodium whole-wheat bread, crumbled.
2 tsp. olive oil.

Directions:

1. In a small bowl, mix the mustard and lemon juice. Spread this evenly over the fillets. Place them in the air fryer basket.
2. In another small bowl, mix the thyme, marjoram, pepper, bread crumbs, and olive oil. Mix until combined.
3. Gently but firmly press the spice mixture onto the top of each fish fillet.
4. Bake at 320°F (160°C) for 8 to 11 minutes, or until the fish reaches an internal temperature of at least 145°F (63°C) on a meat thermometer and the topping is browned and crisp. Serve immediately.

Nutrition:

Calories: 143.
Fat: 4 g.
Protein: 20 g.
Carbs: 5 g.
Fiber: 1 g.
Sugar: 1 g.
Sodium: 140 mg.

33. ALMOND CRUSTED COD WITH CHIPS

Preparation Time:
10'

Cooking Time:
11-15'

Serving:
4

Directions:

1. Preheat the oven to warm.
2. Put the potato slices in the air fryer basket and air fry at 390°F (199°C) for 11 to 15 minutes, or until crisp and brown. With tongs, turn the fries twice during cooking.
3. Meanwhile, in a shallow bowl, beat the egg white and lemon juice until frothy.
4. On a plate, mix the almonds, bread crumbs, and basil.
5. One at a time, dip the fillets into the egg white mixture and then into the almond-bread crumb mixture to coat. Place the coated fillets on a wire rack to dry while the fries cook.
6. When the potatoes are done, transfer them to a baking sheet and keep warm in the oven on low heat.
7. Air fry the fish in the air fryer basket for 10 to 14 minutes, or until the fish reaches an internal temperature of at least 140°F (60°C) on a meat thermometer and the coating is browned and crisp. Serve immediately with the potatoes.

Ingredients:

2 russet potatoes, peeled, thinly sliced, rinsed, and patted dry.
1 egg white.
1 tbsp. freshly squeezed lemon juice.
⅓ cup ground almonds.
2 slices low-sodium whole-wheat bread, finely crumbled.
½ tsp. dried basil.
4 (4-oz. / 113-g) cod fillets.

Nutrition:

Calories: 248.
Fat: 5 g.
Protein: 27 g.
Carbs: 25 g.
Fiber: 3 g.
Sugar: 3 g.
Sodium: 131 mg.

34. STEVIA LEMON SNAPPER WITH FRUIT

Preparation Time: 15'

Cooking Time: 9-13'

Serving: 4

Ingredients:

4 (4-oz. / 113-g) red snapper fillets.
2 tsp. olive oil.
3 nectarines, halved and pitted.
3 plums, halved and pitted.
1 cup red grapes.
1 tbsp. freshly squeezed lemon juice.
1 tbsp. stevia.
½ tsp. dried thyme.

Directions:

1. Put the red snapper in the air fryer basket and drizzle with the olive oil. Air fry at 390°F (199°C) for 4 minutes.
2. Remove the basket and add the nectarines and plums. Scatter the grapes over all.
3. Drizzle with the lemon juice and stevia and sprinkle with the thyme.
4. Return the basket to the air fryer and air fry for 5 to 9 minutes more, or until the fish flakes when tested with a fork and the fruit is tender. Serve immediately.

Nutrition:

Calories: 246.
Fat: 4g.
Protein: 25g.
Carbs: 28g.
Fiber: 3g.
Sugar: 24g.
Sodium: 73mg.

35. Easy Tuna Wraps

Preparation Time: 10'

Cooking Time: 4-7'

Serving: 4

Directions:

1. In a medium bowl, mix the tuna, ginger, garlic, and sesame oil. Let it stand for 10 minutes, then transfer to the air fryer basket.
2. Air fry at 390°F (199°C) for 4 to 7 minutes, or until done to your liking and lightly browned.
3. Make wraps with tuna, tortillas, mayonnaise, lettuce, and bell pepper. Serve immediately.

Ingredients:

1 pound (454 g) fresh tuna steak, cut into 1-inch cubes.
1 tbsp. grated fresh ginger.
2 garlic cloves, minced.
½ tsp. toasted sesame oil.
4 low-sodium whole-wheat tortillas.
¼ cup low-fat mayonnaise.
2 cups shredded romaine lettuce.
1 red bell pepper, thinly sliced.

Nutrition:

Calories: 289.
Fat: 7 g.
Protein: 31 g.
Carbs: 26 g.
Fiber: 1 g.
Sugar: 1 g.
Sodium: 135 mg.

36. ASIAN-INSPIRED SWORDFISH STEAKS

Preparation Time: 10'

Cooking Time: 6-11'

Serving: 4

Ingredients:

4 (4-oz. / 113-g) swordfish steaks.
½ tsp. toasted sesame oil.
1 jalapeño pepper, finely minced.
2 garlic cloves, grated.
1 tbsp. grated fresh ginger.
½ tsp. Chinese five-spice powder.
⅛ tsp. freshly ground black pepper.
2 tbsp. freshly squeezed lemon juice.

Directions:

1. Place the swordfish steaks on a work surface and drizzle with the sesame oil.
2. In a small bowl, mix the jalapeño, garlic, ginger, five-spice powder, pepper, and lemon juice. Rub this mixture into the fish and let it stand for 10 minutes. Put in the air fryer basket.
3. Roast at 380°F (193°C) for 6 to 11 minutes, or until the swordfish reaches an internal temperature of at least 140°F (60°C) on a meat thermometer. Serve immediately.

Nutrition:

Calories: 188.
Fat: 6 g.
Protein: 29 g.
Carbs: 2 g.
Fiber: 0 g.
Sugar: 1 g.
Sodium: 132 mg.

37. SALMON WITH FENNEL AND CARROT

Preparation Time: 15'

Cooking Time: 13-14'

Serving: 2

Directions:

1. Combine the fennel, carrot, and onion in a bowl and toss.
2. Put the vegetable mixture into a baking pan. Roast in the air fryer at 400°F (204°C) for 4 minutes or until the vegetables are crisp-tender.
3. Remove the pan from the air fryer. Stir in the sour cream and sprinkle the vegetables with the pepper.
4. Top with the salmon fillets.
5. Return the pan to the air fryer. Roast for another 9 to 10 minutes or until the salmon just barely flakes when tested with a fork.

Ingredients:

1 fennel bulb, thinly sliced.
1 large carrot, peeled and sliced.
1 small onion, thinly sliced.
¼ cup low-fat sour cream.
¼ tsp. coarsely ground pepper.
2 (5-oz. / 142-g) salmon fillets.

Nutrition:

Calories: 254.
Fat: 9 g.
Protein: 31 g.
Carbs: 12 g.
Fiber: 3 g.
Sugar: 5 g.
Sodium: 115 mg.

38. RANCH TILAPIA FILLETS

Preparation Time: 7'

Cooking Time: 17'

Serving: 2 Fillets

Ingredients:

2 tbsp. flour.
1 egg, lightly beaten.
1 cup crushed cornflakes.
2 tbsp. ranch seasoning.
2 tilapia fillets.
Olive oil spray.

Directions:

1. Place a parchment liner in the air fryer basket.
2. Scoop the flour out onto a plate; set it aside.
3. Put the beaten egg in a medium shallow bowl.
4. Place the cornflakes in a zip-top bag and crush with a rolling pin or another small, blunt object.
5. On another plate, mix to combine the crushed cereal and ranch seasoning.
6. Dredge the tilapia fillets in the flour, then dip in the egg, and then press into the cornflake mixture.
7. Place the prepared fillets on the liner in the air fryer in a single layer.
8. Spray lightly with olive oil, and air fry at 400°F (204°C) for 8 minutes. Carefully flip the fillets, and spray with more oil. Air fry for an additional 9 minutes, until golden and crispy, and serve.

Nutrition:

Calories: 395.
Fat: 7 g.
Protein: 34 g.
Carbs: 49 g.
Fiber: 3 g.
Sugar: 4 g.
Sodium: 980 mg.

39. CHILEAN SEA BASS WITH GREEN OLIVE RELISH

Preparation Time: 10'

Cooking Time: 10'

Serving: 2

Directions:

1. Spray the air fryer basket with the olive oil spray. Drizzle the fillets with the olive oil and sprinkle with the cumin, salt, and pepper. Place the fish in the air fryer basket. Bake at 325°F (163°C) for 10 minutes, or until the fish flakes easily with a fork.
2. Meanwhile, in a small bowl, stir together the olives, onion, and capers.
3. Serve the fish topped with the relish.

Ingredients:

Olive oil spray.
2 (6-oz. / 170-g) Chilean sea bass fillets or other firm-fleshed white fish.
3 tbsp. extra-virgin olive oil.
½ tsp. ground cumin.
½ tsp. kosher salt.
½ tsp. black pepper.
⅓ cup pitted green olives, diced.
¼ cup finely diced onion.
1 tsp. chopped capers.

Nutrition:

Calories: 366.
Fat: 26g.
Protein: 31g.
Carbs: 2g.
Fiber: 1g.
Sugar: 0g.
Sodium: 895mg.

40. GINGER AND GREEN ONION FISH

Preparation Time: 15'

Cooking Time: 15'

Serving: 2

Ingredients:

Bean sauce:
2 tbsp. low-sodium soy sauce.
1 tbsp. rice wine.
1 tbsp. doubanjiang (Chinese black bean paste).
1 tsp. minced fresh ginger.
1 clove garlic, minced.

Vegetables and fish:
1 tbsp. peanut oil.
¼ cup julienned green onions (white and green parts).
¼ cup chopped fresh cilantro.
2 tbsp. julienned fresh ginger.
2 (6-oz. / 170-g) white fish fillets, such as tilapia.

Directions:

1. For the sauce: in a small bowl, combine all the ingredients and stir until well combined; set aside.
2. For the vegetables and fish: in a medium bowl, combine the peanut oil, green onions, cilantro, and ginger. Toss to combine.
3. Cut two squares of parchment large enough to hold one fillet and half of the vegetables. Place one fillet on each parchment square, top with the vegetables, and pour over the sauce. Fold over the parchment paper and crimp the sides in small, tight folds to hold the fish, vegetables, and sauce securely inside the packet.
4. Place the packets in a single layer in the air fryer basket. Roast at 350°F (177°C) for 15 minutes.
5. Transfer each packet to a dinner plate. Cut open with scissors just before serving.

Nutrition:

Calories: 237.
Fat: 9 g.
Protein: 36 g.
Carbs: 3 g.
Fiber: 0 g.
Sugar: 0 g.
Sodium: 641 mg.

41. ASIAN SESAME COD

Preparation Time: 5'

Cooking Time: 7-9'

Serving: 1

Directions:

1. In a small bowl, combine the soy sauce and stevia.
2. Spray the air fryer basket with nonstick cooking spray, then place the cod in the basket, brush with the soy mixture, and sprinkle sesame seeds on top. Roast at 360°F (182°C) for 7 to 9 minutes or until opaque.
3. Remove the fish from the fryer and allow to cool on a wire rack for 5 minutes before serving.

Ingredients:

1 tbsp. reduced-sodium soy sauce.
2 tsp. stevia.
1 tsp. sesame seeds.
6 oz. (170 g) cod fillet.

Nutrition:

Calories: 141.
Fat: 1 g.
Protein: 26 g.
Carbs: 7 g.
Fiber: 1 g.
Sugar: 6 g.
Sodium: 466 mg.

42. ROASTED SHRIMP AND VEGGIES

Preparation Time: 12'	**Cooking Time:** 25-28'	**Serving:** 3 Cups

Ingredients:

Veggies:
½ tsp. salt.
½ tsp. paprika.
¼ tsp. garlic powder.
¼ tsp. ground black pepper.
½ medium zucchini, diced.
1 cup broccoli florets.
½ sweet onion, cut into large chunks.
½ red bell pepper, cut into large chunks.
1 small carrot, sliced thin.
2 small red potatoes, diced.
1 tbsp. olive oil.
1 tbsp. white wine vinegar.

Shrimp:
½ pound (227 g) raw shrimp, peeled and deveined.
1 tbsp. olive oil.
¼ tsp. salt.
¼ tsp. paprika.
¼ tsp. garlic powder.
¼ tsp. ground black pepper.
1 tbsp. lemon juice.

Nutrition:

Calories: 129.
Fat: 5 g.
Protein: 9 g.
Carbs: 12 g.
Fiber: 1 g.
Sugar: 2 g.
Sodium: 352 mg.

Directions:

Make the veggies:
1. In a small bowl, combine the salt, paprika, garlic powder, and pepper. Set aside.
2. In a large bowl, combine the zucchini, broccoli, onion, bell pepper, carrot, and red potatoes.
3. Drizzle the olive oil and white wine vinegar over the veggies, and sprinkle with the spice mixture.
4. Transfer to the air fryer basket and roast at 400°F (204°C) for 15 minutes, or until the veggies are fork-tender.

Make the shrimp:
5. In a large bowl, toss together the shrimp, olive oil, salt, paprika, garlic powder, and pepper.
6. Once the veggies are done roasting, transfer the shrimp mixture to the air fryer basket and roast at 350°F (177°C) for 10 to 13 minutes, or until the shrimp are browned.
7. Toss the shrimp with the roasted veggies and drizzle with the lemon juice before serving.

43. LEMON SCALLOPS WITH ASPARAGUS

Preparation Time:
10'

Cooking Time:
7-10'

Serving:
4

Directions:

1. Place the asparagus snap peas in the air fryer basket. Air fry at 400°F (204°C) for 2 to 3 minutes or until the vegetables are just starting to get tender.
2. Meanwhile, check the scallops for a small muscle attached to the side, and pull it off and discard.
3. In a medium bowl, toss the scallops with the lemon juice, olive oil, thyme, salt, and pepper. Place into the air fryer basket on top of the vegetables.
4. Air fry for 5 to 7 minutes, tossing the basket once during cooking time until the scallops are just firm when tested with your finger and are opaque in the center, and the vegetables are tender. Serve immediately.

Ingredients:

½ pound (227 g) asparagus, ends trimmed and cut into 2-inch pieces.
1 pound (454 g) sea scallops.
1 tbsp. lemon juice.
2 tsp. olive oil.
½ tsp. dried thyme.
Pinch salt.
Freshly ground black pepper, to taste.

Nutrition:

Calories: 163.
Fat: 4g.
Protein: 22g.
Carbs: 10g.
Fiber: 3g.
Sugar: 3g.
Sodium: 225mg.

44. Fish Tacos

Preparation Time: 15'

Cooking Time: 9-12'

Serving: 4

Ingredients:

- 1 pound (454 g) white fish fillets, such as snapper.
- 1 tbsp. olive oil.
- 3 tbsp. freshly squeezed lemon juice, divided.
- 1½ cups chopped red cabbage.
- ½ cup salsa.
- ⅓ cup sour cream.
- 6 whole-wheat tortillas.
- 2 avocados, peeled and chopped.

Directions:

1. Brush the fish with olive oil and sprinkle with 1 tbsp. of the lemon juice. Place in the air fryer basket and air fry at 400°F (204°C) for 9 to 12 minutes or until the fish just flakes when tested with a fork.
2. Meanwhile, combine the remaining 2 tbsp. lemon juice, cabbage, salsa, and sour cream in a medium bowl.
3. When the fish is cooked, remove it from the air fryer basket and break it into large pieces.
4. Let everyone assemble their own taco combining the fish, tortillas, cabbage mixture, and avocados.

Nutrition:

Calories: 547.
Fat: 27 g.
Protein: 33 g.
Carbs: 43 g.
Fiber: 12 g.
Sugar: 4 g.
Sodium: 679 mg.

45. SPICY CAJUN SHRIMP

Preparation Time:
7'

Cooking Time:
10-13'

Serving:
2 Cups

Directions:

1. In a large bowl, combine the shrimp, olive oil, cayenne pepper, Old Bay seasoning, paprika, and salt; toss to combine.
2. Transfer to the air fryer basket and roast at 390°F (199°C) for 10 to 13 minutes, until browned.
3. Drizzle a bit of lemon juice over the shrimp before serving.

Ingredients:

½ pound (227 g) shrimp, peeled and deveined.
1 tbsp. olive oil.
1 tsp. ground cayenne pepper.
½ tsp. Old Bay seasoning.
½ tsp. paprika.
⅛ tsp. salt.
Juice of half a lemon.

Nutrition:

Calories: 159.
Fat: 7 g.
Protein: 23 g.
Carbs: 1 g.
Fiber: 0 g.
Sugar: 0 g.
Sodium: 291 mg.

46. GARLIC PARMESAN ROASTED SHRIMP

Preparation Time:
7'

Cooking Time:
10-13'

Serving:
4 Cups

Ingredients:

1 pound (454 g) jumbo shrimp, peeled and deveined.
1/3 cup parmesan cheese.
1 tbsp. olive oil.
1 tsp. onion powder.
2 tsp. minced garlic.
1/2 tsp. ground black pepper.
1/4 tsp. dried basil.

Directions:

1. In a large bowl, toss to combine the shrimp, parmesan cheese, olive oil, onion powder, garlic, pepper, and basil.
2. Transfer to the air fryer basket and roast at 350°F (177°C) for 10 to 13 minutes, until the shrimp are browned, and serve.

Nutrition:

Calories: 162.
Fat: 6 g.
Protein: 25 g.
Carbs: 2 g.
Fiber: 0 g.
Sugar: 0 g.
Sodium: 271mg.

47. QUICK SHRIMP SCAMPI

Preparation Time: 10'

Cooking Time: 7-8'

Serving: 2

Directions:

1. Spray a baking pan with nonstick cooking spray, then combine the shrimp, olive oil, sliced garlic, lemon juice and zest, kosher salt, and red pepper flakes (if using) in the pan, tossing to coat. Place in the air fryer basket.
2. Roast at 360°F (182°C) for 7 to 8 minutes or until firm and bright pink.
3. Remove the shrimp from the fryer, place it on a serving plate, and sprinkle the parsley on top. Serve warm.

Ingredients:

30 (1 pound / 454 g) uncooked large shrimp, peeled, deveined, and tails removed.
2 tsp. olive oil.
1 garlic clove, thinly sliced.
Juice and zest of ½ lemon.
⅛ tsp. kosher salt.
Pinch of red pepper flakes (optional).
1 tbsp. chopped fresh parsley.

Nutrition:

Calories: 321.
Fat: 13 g.
Protein: 46 g.
Carbs: 5 g.
Fiber: 0 g.
Sugar: 1 g.
Sodium: 383 mg.

48. PORK SPARE RIBS

Preparation Time: 15'

Cooking Time: 20'

Serving: 6

Ingredients:

5-6 garlic cloves, minced.
½ cup of rice vinegar.
2 tbsp. of soy sauce.
Salt and ground black pepper, as required.
12: 1-inch pork spare ribs.
½ cup of cornstarch.
2 tbsp. of olive oil.

Directions:

1. In an enormous bowl, mix the garlic, vinegar, soy sauce, salt, and black pepper.
2. Add the ribs and generously coat with mixture.
3. Refrigerate to marinate overnight.
4. In a shallow bowl, place the cornstarch.
5. Coat the ribs evenly with cornstarch and then, drizzle with oil.
6. Set the temperature of the Air Fryer to 390°F. Grease an Air Fryer basket.
7. Arrange ribs into the prepared Air Fryer basket in a single layer.
8. Air fry for about 10 minutes per side.
9. Remove from Air Fryer and transfer the ribs onto serving plates.
10. Serve immediately.

Nutrition:

Calories: 557.
Carbs: 11g.
Protein: 35g.
Fat: 51.3g.
Sugar: 0.1g.
Sodium: 997mg.

49. BBQ PORK RIBS

Preparation Time: 15'

Cooking Time: 26'

Serving: 4

Directions:

1. In a basin, mix 3 tbsp. of stevia and the remaining ingredients except for pork ribs.
2. Add the pork ribs and generously coat with the mixture.
3. Refrigerate to marinate for about 20 minutes.
4. Set the temperature of the Air Fryer to 355°F. Grease an Air Fryer basket.
5. Arrange ribs into the prepared Air Fryer basket in a single layer.
6. Air fry for about 13 minutes per side.
7. Remove from Air Fryer and transfer the ribs onto plates.
8. Drizzle with the remaining stevia and serve immediately.

NOTE: Worcestershire sauce. The other ingredients that make up this savory sauce usually include onions, molasses, and high fructose corn syrup: depending on the country of production), salt, garlic, tamarind, cloves, chili pepper extract, water and natural flavorings.

Ingredients:

¼ cup of stevia, divided.
¾ cup of BBQ sauce.
2 tbsp. of tomato ketchup.
1 tbsp. of Worcestershire sauce.
1 tbsp. of soy sauce.
½ tsp. of garlic powder.
Freshly ground white pepper to taste.
1¾ pounds of pork ribs.

Nutrition:

Calories: 691.
Carbs: 37.7g.
Protein: 53.1g.
Fat: 31.3g.
Sugar: 32.2g.
Sodium: 991mg.

Chapter 5
DIABETIC AIR FRYER MEAT RECIPES

50. ROASTED VEGETABLE AND CHICKEN SALAD

Preparation Time: 10'

Cooking Time: 10-13'

Serving: 4

Ingredients:

3 boneless, skinless chicken breasts, cut into 1-inch cubes.
1 small red onion, sliced.
1 orange bell pepper, sliced.
1 cup sliced yellow summer squash.
4 tbsp. stevia mustard salad dressing, divided.
½ tsp. dried thyme.
½ cup mayonnaise.
2 tbsp. freshly squeezed lemon juice.

Directions:

1. Place the chicken, onion, pepper, and squash in the air fryer basket. Drizzle with 1 tbsp. of the stevia mustard salad dressing, add the thyme, and toss.
2. Roast at 400°F (204°C) for 10 to 13 minutes or until the chicken is 165°F (74°C) on a food thermometer, tossing the food once during cooking time.
3. Transfer the chicken and vegetables to a bowl and mix in the remaining 3 tbsp. of stevia mustard salad dressing, mayonnaise and lemon juice. Serve on lettuce leaves, if desired.

Nutrition:

Calories: 495.
Fat: 23 g.
Protein: 51 g.
Carbs: 18 g.
Fiber: 2 g.
Sugar: 5 g.
Sodium: 439 mg.

51. CHICKEN SATAY

Preparation Time:
12'

Cooking Time:
12-18'

Serving:
4

Directions:

1. In a medium bowl, combine the peanut butter, chicken broth, soy sauce, lemon juice, garlic, olive oil, and curry powder, and mix well with a wire whisk until smooth. Remove 2 tbsp. of this mixture to a small bowl. Put the remaining sauce into a serving bowl and set aside.
2. Add the chicken tenders to the bowl with the 2-tbsp. sauce and stir to coat. Let stand for a few minutes to marinate, then run a bamboo skewer through each chicken tender lengthwise.
3. Put the chicken in the air fryer basket and air fry in batches at 390°F (199°C) for 6 to 9 minutes or until the chicken reaches 165°F (74°C) on a meat thermometer. Serve the chicken with the reserved sauce.

Ingredients:

½ cup crunchy peanut butter.
⅓ cup chicken broth.
3 tbsp. low-sodium soy sauce.
2 tbsp. freshly squeezed lemon juice.
2 cloves garlic, minced.
2 tbsp. olive oil.
1 tsp. curry powder.
1 pound (454 g) chicken tenders.

Nutrition:

Calories: 449.
Fat: 28 g.
Protein: 46 g.
Carbs: 8 g.
Fiber: 2 g.
Sugar: 3 g.
Sodium: 984 mg.

52. CHICKEN FAJITAS WITH AVOCADOS

Preparation Time:
10'

Cooking Time:
10-14'

Serving:
4

Ingredients:

4 boneless, skinless chicken breasts, sliced.
1 small red onion, sliced.
2 red bell peppers, sliced.
½ cup spicy ranch salad dressing, divided.
½ tsp. dried oregano.
8 corn tortillas.
2 cups torn butter lettuce.
2 avocados, peeled and chopped.

Directions:

1. Place the chicken, onion, and pepper in the air fryer basket. Drizzle with 1 tbsp. of the salad dressing and add the oregano. Toss to combine.
2. Air fry at 380°F (193°C) for 10 to 14 minutes or until the chicken is 165°F (74°C) on a food thermometer.
3. Transfer the chicken and vegetables to a bowl and toss with the remaining salad dressing.
4. Serve the chicken mixture with the tortillas, lettuce, and avocados and let everyone make their own creations.

Nutrition:

Calories: 784.
Fat: 38 g.
Protein: 72 g.
Carbs: 39 g.
Fiber: 12 g.
Sugar: 4 g.
Sodium: 397 mg.

53. CRISPY BUTTERMILK FRIED CHICKEN

Preparation Time: 7'

Cooking Time: 20-25'

Serving: 4

Directions:

1. Pat the chicken dry. In a shallow bowl, combine the flour, paprika, salt, and pepper.
2. In another bowl, beat the buttermilk with the eggs until smooth.
3. In a third bowl, combine the olive oil and bread crumbs until mixed.
4. Dredge the chicken in the flour, then into the eggs to coat, and finally into the bread crumbs, patting the crumbs firmly onto the chicken skin.
5. Air fry the chicken at 370°F (188°C) for 20 to 25 minutes, turning each piece over halfway during cooking until the meat registers 165°F (74°C) on a meat thermometer and the chicken is brown and crisp. Let cool for 5 minutes, then serve.

Ingredients:

6 chicken pieces: drumsticks, breasts, and thighs.
1 cup flour.
2 tsp. paprika.
Pinch salt.
Freshly ground black pepper, to taste.
⅓ cup buttermilk.
2 eggs.
2 tbsp. olive oil.
1½ cups bread crumbs.

Nutrition:

Calories: 645.
Fat: 17 g.
Protein: 62 g.
Carbs: 55 g.
Fiber: 3 g.
Sugar: 5 g.
Sodium: 495 mg.

54. GARLICKY CHICKEN WITH CREAMER POTATOES

Preparation Time: 10'

Cooking Time: 25'

Serving: 4

Ingredients:

1 (2½- to 3-pound / 1.1- to 1.4-kg) broiler-fryer whole chicken.
2 tbsp. olive oil.
½ tsp. garlic salt.
8 cloves garlic, peeled.
1 slice lemon.
½ tsp. dried thyme.
½ tsp. dried marjoram.
12 to 16 creamer potatoes, scrubbed.

Directions:

1. Do not wash the chicken before cooking. Remove it from its packaging and pat the chicken dry.
2. Combine the olive oil and salt in a small bowl. Rub half of this mixture on the inside of the chicken, under the skin, and on the chicken skin. Place the garlic cloves and the lemon slice inside the chicken. Sprinkle the chicken with the thyme and marjoram.
3. Put the chicken in the air fryer basket. Surround with the potatoes and drizzle the potatoes with the remaining olive oil mixture.
4. Roast at 380°F (193°C) for 25 minutes, then test the temperature of the chicken. It should be 160°F (71°C). Test at the thickest part of the breast, making sure the probe doesn't touch bone. If the chicken isn't done yet, return it to the air fryer and roast it for 4 to 5 minutes, or until the temperature is 160°F (71°C).
5. When the chicken is done, transfer it and the potatoes to a serving platter and cover it with foil. Let the chicken rest for 5 minutes before serving.

Nutrition:

Calories: 492.
Fat: 14 g.
Protein: 68 g.
Carbs: 20 g.
Fiber: 3 g.
Sugar: 1 g.
Sodium: 151 mg.

Melissa Simson

55. BAKED CHICKEN CORDON BLEU

Preparation Time: 15'

Cooking Time: 13-15'

Serving: 4

Directions:

1. Put the chicken breast fillets on a work surface and gently press them with the palm of your hand to make them a bit thinner. Don't tear the meat.
2. In a small bowl, combine the ham and cheese. Divide this mixture among the chicken fillets. Wrap the chicken around the filling to enclose it, using toothpicks to hold the chicken together.
3. In a shallow bowl, mix the flour, salt, pepper, and marjoram. In another bowl, beat the egg. Spread the bread crumbs out on a plate.
4. Dip the chicken into the flour mixture, then into the egg, then into the bread crumbs to coat thoroughly.
5. Put the chicken in the air fryer basket and mist with olive oil.
6. Bake at 380°F (193°C) for 13 to 15 minutes or until the chicken is thoroughly cooked to 165°F (74°C). Carefully remove the toothpicks and serve.

Ingredients:

4 chicken breast fillets.
¼ cup chopped ham.
⅓ cup grated Swiss or Gruyère cheese.
¼ cup flour.
Pinch salt.
Freshly ground black pepper, to taste.
½ tsp. dried marjoram.
1 egg.
1 cup whole-wheat bread crumbs.
Olive oil for misting.

Nutrition:

Calories: 479.
Fat: 12 g.
Protein: 64 g.
Carbs: 26 g.
Fiber: 2 g.
Sugar: 0 g.
Sodium: 575 mg.

56. CHICKEN TENDERS AND VEGETABLES

Preparation Time:
10'

Cooking Time:
18-20'

Serving:
4

Ingredients:

1 pound (454 g) chicken tenders.
1 tbsp. stevia.
Pinch salt.
Freshly ground black pepper, to taste.
½ cup soft fresh bread crumbs.
½ tsp. dried thyme.
1 tbsp. olive oil.
2 carrots, sliced.
12 small red potatoes.

Directions:

1. In a medium bowl, toss the chicken tenders with stevia, salt, and pepper.
2. In a shallow bowl, combine the bread crumbs, thyme, and olive oil, and mix.
3. Coat the tenders in the bread crumbs, pressing firmly onto the meat.
4. Place the carrots and potatoes in the air fryer basket and top with the chicken tenders.
5. Roast at 380°F (193°C) for 18 to 20 minutes or until the chicken is cooked to 165°F (74°C) and the vegetables are tender, shaking the basket halfway during the cooking time.

Nutrition:

Calories: 379.
Fat: 8 g.
Protein: 41 g.
Carbs: 35 g.
Fiber: 3 g.
Sugar: 9 g.
Sodium: 296 mg.

57. GREEK CHICKEN KEBABS

Preparation Time:
15'

Cooking Time:
15'

Serving:
4

Directions:

1. In a large bowl, whisk the lemon juice, olive oil, parsley, oregano, and mint.
2. Add the chicken and stir to coat. Let stand for 10 minutes at room temperature.
3. Alternating the items, thread the chicken, tomatoes, and squash onto 8 bamboo or metal skewers that fit in an air fryer. Brush with marinade.
4. Air fry the kebabs at 380°F (193°C) for about 15 minutes, brushing once with any remaining marinade until the chicken reaches an internal temperature of 165°F (74°C) on a meat thermometer. Discard any remaining marinade. Serve immediately.

Ingredients:

3 tbsp. freshly squeezed lemon juice.
2 tsp. olive oil.
2 tbsp. chopped fresh flat-leaf parsley.
½ tsp. dried oregano.
½ tsp. dried mint.
1 pound (454 g) low-sodium boneless, skinless chicken breasts, cut into 1-inch pieces.
1 cup cherry tomatoes.
1 small yellow summer squash, cut into 1-inch cubes.

Nutrition:

Calories: 164.
Fat: 4 g.
Protein: 27 g.
Carbs: 4 g.
Fiber: 1 g.
Sugar: 1 g.
Sodium: 70 mg.

58. TANDOORI CHICKEN

Preparation Time: 5'

Cooking Time: 18-23'

Serving: 4

Ingredients:

⅔ cup plain low-fat yogurt.
2 tbsp. freshly squeezed lemon juice.
2 tsp. curry powder.
½ tsp. ground cinnamon.
2 garlic cloves, minced.
2 tsp. olive oil.
4 (5-oz. / 142-g) low-sodium boneless, skinless chicken breasts.

Directions:

1. In a medium bowl, whisk the yogurt, lemon juice, curry powder, cinnamon, garlic, and olive oil.
2. With a sharp knife, cut thin slashes into the chicken. Add it to the yogurt mixture and turn to coat. Let stand for 10 minutes at room temperature. You can also prepare this ahead of time and marinate the chicken in the refrigerator for up to 24 hours.
3. Remove the chicken from the marinade and shake off any excess liquid. Discard any remaining marinade.
4. Roast the chicken at 360°F (182°C) for 10 minutes. With tongs, carefully turn each piece. Roast for 8 to 13 minutes more, or until the chicken reaches an internal temperature of 165°F (74°C) on a meat thermometer. Serve immediately.

Nutrition:

Calories: 198.
Fat: 5 g.
Protein: 33 g.
Carbs: 4 g.
Fiber: 0 g.
Sugar: 3 g.
Sodium: 93 mg.

Melissa Simson

59. STEVIA LEMON GARLIC CHICKEN

Preparation Time:
10'

Cooking Time:
16-19'

Serving:
4

Directions:

1. In a large bowl, mix the chicken and olive oil. Sprinkle with the cornstarch. Toss to coat.
2. Add the garlic and transfer to a baking pan. Bake in the air fryer at 400°F (204°C) for 10 minutes, stirring once during cooking.
3. Add the chicken broth, lemon juice, stevia, and thyme to the chicken mixture. Bake for 6 to 9 minutes more, or until the sauce is slightly thickened and the chicken reaches an internal temperature of 165°F (74°C) on a meat thermometer. Serve over hot cooked brown rice, if desired.

Ingredients:

4 (5-oz. / 142-g) low-sodium boneless, skinless chicken breasts, cut into 4-by-½-inch strips.
2 tsp. olive oil.
2 tbsp. cornstarch.
3 garlic cloves, minced.
½ cup low-sodium chicken broth.
¼ cup freshly squeezed lemon juice.
1 tbsp. stevia.
½ tsp. dried thyme.
Brown rice, cooked (optional).

Nutrition:

Calories: 214.
Fat: 4 g.
Protein: 33 g.
Carbs: 10 g.
Fiber: 0 g.
Sugar: 5 g.
Sodium: 100 mg.

60. BAKED LEMON PEPPER CHICKEN DRUMSTICKS

Preparation Time: 5'

Cooking Time: 22'

Serving: 6 Drumsticks

Ingredients:

Olive oil spray.
6 chicken drumsticks.
1 tsp. lemon pepper.
½ tsp. salt.
½ tsp. granulated garlic.
½ tsp. onion powder.

Directions:

1. Spray the chicken with olive oil and spray the air fryer basket or line it with parchment paper.
2. In a small bowl, combine the lemon pepper, salt, garlic, and onion powder.
3. Place the chicken in the prepared air fryer basket, and sprinkle with half of the seasoning mixture.
4. Bake at 370°F (188°C) for 10 minutes.
5. Flip the drumsticks, and spray them with more olive oil and sprinkle with the remaining seasoning.
6. Place the chicken back in the air fryer, bake for an additional 12 minutes, and serve.
7. The chicken is done when the internal temperature reaches 180°F (82°C) and the juices run clear. It should look slightly crisp on the outside.

Nutrition:

Calories: 195.
Fat: 11 g.
Protein: 23 g.
Carbs: 1 g.
Fiber: 0 g.
Sugar: 0 g.
Sodium: 332 mg.

61. BALSAMIC GLAZED CHICKEN

Preparation Time: 5'

Cooking Time: 22'

Serving: 4 Thighs

Directions:

Make the glaze:
1. In a small bowl, whisk together the olive oil, balsamic vinegar, garlic, stevia, cornstarch, salt, and pepper. Set aside.

Make the chicken:
2. Spray the chicken and the air fryer basket with olive oil.
3. Place the chicken in the air fryer basket, and sprinkle with about half of the garlic, salt, pepper, and onion powder.
4. Bake at 380°F (193°C) for 10 minutes.
5. Remove the chicken and flip the pieces. Spray it with more olive oil, and sprinkle with the remaining seasoning.
6. Place the chicken back in the air fryer and bake for an additional 10 minutes.
7. Remove the chicken, and brush with the prepared glaze. Bake for an additional 2 minutes, or until the sauce is sticky and caramelized, and serve.

Ingredients:

Glaze:
1 tbsp. olive oil.
2 tsp. balsamic vinegar.
1 tsp. minced garlic.
1 tsp. stevia.
½ tsp. cornstarch.
¼ tsp. salt.
¼ tsp. ground black pepper.

Chicken:
Olive oil spray.
4 bone-in chicken thighs.
2 tsp. granulated garlic, divided.
1 tsp. salt, divided.
½ tsp. ground black pepper, divided.
¼ tsp. onion powder, divided.

Nutrition:

Calories: 263.
Fat: 11 g.
Protein: 38 g.
Carbs: 3 g.
Fiber: 0 g.
Sugar: 1 g.
Sodium: 911 mg.

62. HARISSA ROASTED CORNISH GAME HENS

Preparation Time: 10'

Cooking Time: 21'

Serving: 4

Ingredients:

Harissa:
½ cup olive oil.
6 cloves garlic, minced.
2 tbsp. smoked paprika.
1 tbsp. ground coriander.
1 tbsp. ground cumin.
1 tsp. ground caraway.
1 tsp. kosher salt.
½ to 1 tsp. cayenne pepper.

Hens:
½ cup yogurt.
2 Cornish game hens, any giblets removed and split in half lengthwise.

Directions:

1. **For the harissa:** in a medium microwave-safe bowl, combine the oil, garlic, paprika, coriander, cumin, caraway, salt, and cayenne. Microwave on high for 1 minute, stirring halfway through the cooking time. You can also heat this on the stovetop until the oil is hot and bubbling. Or, if you must use your air fryer for everything, air fry it in the air fryer at 350°F (177°C) for 5 to 6 minutes, or until the paste is heated through.
2. **For the hens:** in a small bowl, combine 1 to 2 tbsp. harissa and the yogurt. Whisk until well combined. Place the hen halves in a resealable plastic bag and pour the marinade over. Seal the bag and massage until all of the pieces are thoroughly coated. Marinate at room temperature for 30 minutes or in the refrigerator for up to 24 hours.
3. Arrange the hen halves in a single layer in the air fryer basket. If you have a smaller air fryer, you may have to cook this in two batches. Roast at 400°F (204°C) for 20 minutes. Use a meat thermometer to ensure the game hens have reached an internal temperature of 165°F (74°C).

Nutrition:

Calories: 412.
Fat: 32 g.
Protein: 26 g.
Carbs: 5 g.
Fiber: 1 g.
Sugar: 1 g.
Sodium: 683 mg.

63. STEVIA MUSTARD TURKEY BREAST

Preparation Time: 5'

Cooking Time: 30'

Serving: 8 Slices

Directions:

1. In a small bowl, whisk well to combine the stevia, olive oil, Dijon mustard, butter, garlic, salt, and pepper.
2. Place the turkey breast in the air fryer basket, and brush with the stevia mixture.
3. Bake at 400°F (204°C) for 20 minutes.
4. Remove the turkey breast, brush it with more of the stevia mixture, and bake for an additional 10 minutes, until golden.
5. Let the turkey rest for 5 to 10 minutes before slicing and serving.

Ingredients:

¼ cup stevia.
¼ cup olive oil.
1 tbsp. Dijon mustard.
1 tbsp. butter, melted.
2 tsp. minced garlic.
1 tsp. salt.
½ tsp. ground black pepper.
2½ pound (1.1 kg) boneless turkey breast.

Nutrition:

Calories: 526.
Fat: 22 g.
Protein: 64 g.
Carbs: 18 g.
Fiber: 0 g.
Sugar: 17 g.
Sodium: 961 mg.

64. SOUTH INDIAN PEPPER CHICKEN

Preparation Time: 20'

Cooking Time: 15'

Serving: 4

Ingredients:

Spice mix:
1 dried red chili, or ½ tsp. dried red pepper flakes.
1-inch piece cinnamon or cassia bark.
1½ tsp. coriander seeds.
1 tsp. fennel seeds.
1 tsp. cumin seeds.
1 tsp. black peppercorns.
½ tsp. cardamom seeds.
¼ tsp. ground turmeric.
1 tsp. kosher salt.

Chicken:
1 pound (454 g) boneless, skinless chicken thighs, cut crosswise into thirds.
2 medium onions, cut into ½-inch-thick slices.
¼ cup olive oil.
Cauliflower rice, steamed rice, or naan bread, for serving.

Nutrition:

Calories: 254.
Fat: 18 g.
Protein: 22 g.
Carbs: 1 g.
Fiber: 0 g.
Sugar: 0 g.
Sodium: 691 mg.

Directions:

1. **For the spice mix:** combine the dried chili, cinnamon, coriander, fennel, cumin, peppercorns, and cardamom in a clean coffee or spice grinder. Grind, shaking the grinder lightly so all the seeds and bits get into the blades until the mixture is broken down to a fine powder. Stir in the turmeric and salt.
2. **For the chicken:** place the chicken and onions in a resealable plastic bag. Add the oil and 1½ tbsp. of the spice mix. Seal the bag and massage until the chicken is well coated. Marinate at room temperature for 30 minutes or in the refrigerator for up to 24 hours.
3. Place the chicken and onions in the air fryer basket. Bake at 350°F (177°C) for 10 minutes, stirring once halfway through the cooking time. Increase the temperature to 400°F (204°C) and bake for 5 minutes more. Use a meat thermometer to ensure the chicken has reached an internal temperature of 165°F (74°C).
4. Serve with steamed rice, cauliflower rice, or naan.

65. MINI TURKEY MEATLOAVES

Preparation Time: 6'

Cooking Time: 20-24'

Serving: 4

Directions:

1. In a medium bowl, stir together the onion, carrot, garlic, almonds, olive oil, marjoram, and egg white.
2. Add the ground turkey. With your hands, gently but thoroughly mix until combined.
3. Double 16 foil muffin cup liners to make 8 cups. Divide the turkey mixture evenly among the liners.
4. Bake at 400°F (204°C) for 20 to 24 minutes, or until the meatloaves reach an internal temperature of 165°F (74°C) on a meat thermometer. Serve immediately.

Ingredients:

⅓ cup minced onion.
¼ cup grated carrot.
2 garlic cloves, minced.
2 tbsp. ground almonds.
2 tsp. olive oil.
1 tsp. dried marjoram.
1 egg white.
¾ pound (340 g) ground turkey breast.

Nutrition:

Calories: 142.
Fat: 5 g.
Protein: 23 g.
Carbs: 3 g.
Fiber: 1 g.
Sugar: 1 g.
Sodium: 61 mg.

Chapter 6
DIABETIC AIR FRYER VEGETABLES AND SIDES

66. EGGPLANT SURPRISE

Preparation Time: 10-20'

Cooking Time: 17'

Serving: 4

Ingredients:

1 eggplant, roughly chopped.
3 zucchinis, roughly chopped.
3 tbsp. of extra virgin olive oil.
3 tomatoes, sliced.
2 tbsp. of lemon juice.
1 tsp. of thyme; dried.
1 tsp. of oregano; dried.
Salt and black pepper to the taste.

Directions:

1. Put eggplant pieces in your instant pot.
2. Add zucchinis and tomatoes.
3. In a bowl, mix lemon juice with salt, pepper, thyme, oregano, and oil and stir well.
4. Pour this over veggies, toss to coat, seal the instant pot lid and cook at High for 7 minutes.
5. Quick-release the pressure, carefully open the lid; divide among plates and serve.

Nutrition:

Calories: 160.
Fat: 7g.
Protein: 1g.
Sugar: 6g.
Carbs: 19g.
Fiber: 8g.
Sodium: 20mg.

67. CARROTS AND TURNIPS

Preparation Time:
10-20'

Cooking Time:
15'

Serving:
4

Directions:

1. Set your instant pot on Sauté mode; add oil and heat it up.
2. Add onion, stir and sauté for 2 minutes.
3. Add turnips, carrots, cumin and lemon juice, stir and cook for 1 minute.
4. Add salt, pepper, and water; then stir well. Close the lid and cook at High for 6 minutes.
5. Quickly release the pressure, open the instant pot lid, and divide turnips and carrots among plates and serve.

Ingredients:

2 turnips, peeled and sliced.
1 small onion; chopped.
1 tsp. of lemon juice.
1 tsp. of cumin, ground.
3 carrots, sliced.
1 tbsp. of extra-virgin olive oil.
1 cup of water.
Salt and black pepper to the taste.

Nutrition:

Calories: 170.
Fat: 9g.
Protein: 1g.
Sugar: 5g.
Carbs: 19g.
Fiber: 7g.
Sodium: 475mg.

68. SHRIMP AND ASPARAGUS

Preparation Time: 10-20'

Cooking Time: 8'

Serving: 4

Ingredients:

1 lb. of shrimp, peeled and deveined.
1 cup of water.
1/2 tbsp. of Cajun seasoning.
1 tsp. of extra virgin olive oil.
1 bunch of asparagus, trimmed.

Directions:

1. Pour the water into your instant pot.
2. Put asparagus in the steamer basket of the pot and add shrimp on top.
3. Drizzle olive oil, sprinkle Cajun seasoning; and then stir well. Close the lid and cook on Low for 2 minutes.
4. Release the pressure naturally, transfer asparagus and shrimp to plates and serve.

Nutrition:

Calories: 200
Fat: 3g.
Protein: 8g.
Sugar: 3g.

69. INSTANT BRUSSELS SPROUTS WITH PARMESAN

Preparation Time:
10-20'

Cooking Time:
16'

Serving:
4

Directions:

1. Put sprouts in your instant pot, add salt, pepper and water; and then stir well. Close the lid and cook at High for 3 minutes.
2. Quick-release the pressure, transfer sprouts to a bowl, discard water and clean your pot.
3. Set your pot on Sauté mode; add butter and melt it. Add lemon juice and stir well.
4. Add sprouts, stir and transfer to plates.
5. Add more salt, pepper if needed, and Parmesan cheese on top.

Ingredients:

1 lb. of Brussels sprouts, washed.
1 cup of water.
3 tbsp. of Parmesan, grated.
Juice of 1 lemon.
2 tbsp. of butter.
Salt and black pepper to the taste.

Nutrition:

Calories: 230.
Fat: 10g.
Protein: 8g.
Sugar: 5g.

70. BRAISED FENNEL

Preparation Time:
10'

Cooking Time:
20'

Serving:
22

Ingredients:

2 fennel bulbs, trimmed and cut into quarters.
3 tbsp. extra virgin olive oil.
1/4 cup of white wine.
1/4 cup of Parmesan cheese, grated.
3/4 cup of veggie stock.
Juice of 1/2 lemon.
1 garlic clove; chopped.
1 dried red pepper.
Salt and black pepper to the taste.

Directions:

1. Set your instant pot on Sauté mode; add oil and heat it up.
2. Add garlic and red pepper; then stir well. Cook for 2 minutes and discard garlic.
3. Add fennel, stir and brown it for 8 minutes.
4. Add salt, pepper, stock, wine, close the lid and cook at High for 4 minutes.
5. Quickly release the pressure, open the instant pot lid, add lemon juice, more salt and pepper if needed, and cheese.
6. Mix to coat, divide among plates and serve.

Nutrition:

Calories: 230.
Fat: 4g.
Protein: 1g.
Sugar: 3g.

71. BRUSSELS SPROUTS & POTATOES DISH

Preparation Time:
10-20'

Cooking Time:
15'

Serving:
4

Directions:

1. In a shallow bowl, whisk the egg with buttermilk.
2. In another bowl, mix the breadcrumbs, cheese, onion powder, and garlic powder.
3. Dip the pickle chips in the egg mixture, then, dredge with the breadcrumb/cheese mixture.
4. Cook in the preheated Air Fryer at 400°F for 5 minutes; shake the basket and cook for 5 minutes more.
5. Meanwhile, mix all the sauce ingredients until well combined. Serve the fried pickles with the mayo sauce for dipping.

Ingredients:

4 bell peppers, seeded and sliced (1-inch pieces).
1 onion, sliced (1-inch pieces).
1 tbsp. of olive oil.
1/2 tsp. of dried rosemary.
1/2 tsp. of dried basil.
Kosher salt, to taste.
1/4 tsp. of ground black pepper.
1/3 cup of mayonnaise.
1/3 tsp. of Sriracha.

Nutrition:

Calories: 342.
Fat: 28.5g.
Carbs: 12.5g.
Protein: 9.1g.
Sugars: 4.9g.

72. BEET AND ORANGE SALAD

Preparation Time:
10-20'

Cooking Time:
20'

Serving:
4

Ingredients:

1 ½ lb. of beets.
3 strips orange peel.
2 tbsp. of cider vinegar.
1/2 cup of orange juice.
2 tsp. of orange zest, grated.
2 scallions; chopped.
2 tsp. of mustard.
2 cups of arugula and mustard greens.

Directions:

1. Scrub beets well, cut them in halves and put them in a bowl.
2. In your instant pot, mix orange peel strips with vinegar and orange juice and stir.
3. Add beets, seal the instant pot lid, cook at High for 7 minutes, and naturally release the pressure.
4. Carefully open the lid, take beets and transfer them to a bowl.
5. Discard peel strips from the pot, add mustard and stir well.
6. Add scallions, grated orange zest to beets, and toss them.
7. Add liquid from the pot over beets, toss to coat and serve on plates on top of mixed salad greens.

Nutrition:

Calories: 164.
Fat: 5g.
Protein: 2g.
Sugar: 5g.

73. ENDIVES DISH

Preparation Time: 10-20'

Cooking Time: 30'

Serving: 4

Directions:

1. Put the endives in the steamer basket of your instant pot, add some water to the pot, cover and cook at High for 10 minutes.
2. Meanwhile, heat up a pan with the butter over medium heat, stir and melt it.
3. Add flour, stir well and cook for 3 minutes.
4. Add milk, salt, pepper and nutmeg, stir well, reduce heat to low and cook for 10 minutes.
5. Release the pressure from the pot, uncover it, transfer them to a cutting board and roll each in a slice of ham.
6. Arrange endives in a pan, add the milk mixture over them, introduce in preheated broiler and broil for 10 minutes. Slice, arrange on plates and serve.

Ingredients:

4 endives, trimmed.
2 tbsp. of butter.
1 tbsp. of white flour.
4 slices ham.
1/2 tsp. of nutmeg.
14 oz. of milk.
Salt and black pepper to taste.

Nutrition:

Calories: 175.
Fat: 8g.
Protein: 1g.
Sugar: 2g.

74. ROASTED POTATOES

Preparation Time:
10-20'

Cooking Time:
30'

Serving:
4

Ingredients:

2 lb. of baby potatoes.
5 tbsp. of vegetable oil.
1/2 cup of stock.
1 rosemary spring.
5 garlic cloves.
Salt and black pepper to the taste.

Directions:

1. Set your instant pot on Sauté mode; add oil and heat it up.
2. Add potatoes, rosemary and garlic, stir and brown them for 10 minutes.
3. Prick each potato with a knife, add the stock, salt and pepper to the pot, Seal the Instant Pot lid and cook at High for 7 minutes.
4. Quickly release the pressure, open the instant pot lid, divide potatoes among plates and serve.

Nutrition:

Calories: 250.
Fat: 15g.
Protein: 2g.
Sugar: 1g.

75. CABBAGE WEDGES

Preparation Time:
10'

Cooking Time:
29'

Serving:
6

Directions:

1. Switch on the Air Fryer, insert the fryer basket, grease it with olive oil, then shut with its lid, set the fryer to 350°F, and preheat for 5 minutes.
2. Open the fryer, add bacon strips in it, close with its lid and cook for 10 minutes until nicely golden and crispy, turning the bacon halfway through the frying.
3. Meanwhile, prepare the cabbage, remove the cabbage's outer leaves, and then cut it into eight wedges, keeping the core intact.
4. Prepare the spice mix and for this, place onion powder in a bowl, add black pepper, garlic powder, salt, red chili, and fennel and stir until mixed.
5. Drizzle cabbage wedges with oil and then sprinkle with spice mix until well coated.
6. When the Air Fryer beeps, open its lid, transfer bacon strips to a cutting board and let it rest.
7. Add seasoned cabbage wedges into the fryer basket, close with its lid, then cook for 8 minutes at 400°F, flip the cabbage, spray with oil and continue air frying for 6 minutes until nicely golden and cooked.
8. When done, transfer cabbage wedges to a plate.
9. Chop the bacon, sprinkle it over cabbage and serve.

Ingredients:

1 small head of green cabbage.
6 strips of bacon, thick-cut, pastured.
1 tsp. of onion powder.
½ tsp. of ground black pepper.
1 tsp. of garlic powder.
¾ tsp. of salt.
1/4 tsp. of red chili flakes.
1/2 tsp. of fennel seeds.
3 tbsp. of olive oil.

Nutrition:

Calories: 123.
Carbs: 2 g.
Fat: 11 g.
Protein: 4 g.
Fiber: 0 g.
Sugar: 1g.

76. BUFFALO CAULIFLOWER WINGS

Preparation Time: 5'

Cooking Time: 30'

Serving: 6

Ingredients:

1 tbsp. of almond flour.
1 medium head of cauliflower.
1 ½ tsp. of salt.
4 tbsp. of hot sauce.
1 tbsp. of olive oil.

Directions:

1. Switch on the Air Fryer, insert the fryer basket, grease it with olive oil, then shut with its lid, set the fryer to 400°F, and preheat for 5 minutes.
2. Meanwhile, cut cauliflower into bite-size florets and set aside.
3. Place flour in a large bowl, whisk in salt, oil, and hot sauce until combined, add cauliflower florets and toss until combined.
4. Open the fryer, add cauliflower florets in it in a single layer, close with its lid and cook for 15 minutes until nicely golden and crispy, shaking halfway through the frying.
5. When the Air Fryer beeps, open its lid, transfer cauliflower florets onto a serving plate and keep warm.
6. Cook the remaining cauliflower florets the same way and serve.

Nutrition:

Calories: 48.
Carbs: 1 g.
Fat: 4 g.
Protein: 1 g.
Fiber: 0.5 g.

77. SWEET POTATO CAULIFLOWER PATTIES

Preparation Time:
20'

Cooking Time:
40'

Serving:
7

Directions:

1. Cut peeled sweet potato into small pieces, then place them in a food processor and pulse until pieces are broken up.
2. Then add onion, cauliflower florets, and garlic, pulse until combined, add remaining ingredients and pulse more until well combined.
3. Tip the mixture in a bowl, shape the mixture into seven 1 ½ inch thick patties, each about ¼ cup, then place them on a baking sheet and freeze for 10 minutes.
4. Switch on the Air Fryer, insert the fryer basket, grease it with olive oil, then shut with its lid, set the fryer at 400°F, and preheat for 10 minutes.
5. Open the fryer, add patties to it in a single layer, close with its lid and cook for 20 minutes until nicely golden and cooked, flipping the patties halfway through the frying.
6. When the Air Fryer beeps, open its lid, transfer patties onto a serving plate, and keep them warm.
7. Prepare the continuing patties the same way and serve.

Ingredients:

1 green onion, chopped.
1 large sweet potato, peeled.
1 tsp. of minced garlic.
1 cup of cilantro leaves.
2 cups of cauliflower florets.
¼ tsp. of ground black pepper.
1/4 tsp. of salt.
1/4 cup of sunflower seeds.
1/4 tsp. of cumin.
1/4 cup of ground flaxseed.
1/2 tsp. of red chili powder.
2 tbsp. of ranch seasoning mix.
2 tbsp. of arrowroot starch.

Nutrition:

Calories: 85.
Carbs: 9 g.
Fat: 3 g.
Protein: 2.7 g.
Fiber: 3.5 g.

78. OKRA

Preparation Time: 10'

Cooking Time: 10'

Serving: 4

Ingredients:

1 cup of almond flour.
8 oz of fresh okra.
1/2 tsp. of sea salt.
1 cup of milk, reduced-fat.
1 egg, pastured.

Directions:

1. Snap the egg in a basin, pour in the milk, and whisk until blended.
2. Cut the stem from each okra, then cut it into ½-inch pieces, add them into the egg and stir until well coated.
3. Mix flour and salt and add it into a large plastic bag.
4. Working on one okra piece at a time, drain the okra well by letting excess egg drip off, add it to the flour mixture, then seal the bag and shake well until okra is well coated.
5. Place the coated okra on a grease Air Fryer basket, coat the remaining okra pieces the same way and place them into the basket.
6. Switch on the Air Fryer, insert the fryer basket, spray okra with oil, then shut with its lid, set the fryer to 390°F, and cook for 10 minutes until nicely golden and cooked, stirring okra halfway through the frying.
7. Serve straight away.

Nutrition:

Calories: 250.
Carbs: 38 g.
Fat: 9 g.
Protein: 3 g.
Fiber: 2 g.

79. CREAMED SPINACH

Preparation Time:
10'

Cooking Time:
20'

Serving:
2

Directions:

1. Switch on the Air Fryer, insert the fryer basket, grease it with olive oil, then shut with its lid, set the fryer at 350°F, and preheat for 5 minutes.
2. Meanwhile, take a 6-inches baking pan, grease it with oil, and set it aside.
3. Put spinach in a basin, add remaining ingredients except for Parmesan cheese, stir until well mixed and then add the mixture into a prepared baking pan.
4. Open the fryer, add pan in it, close with its lid and cook for 10 minutes until cooked and cheese has melted, stirring halfway through.
5. Then sprinkle Parmesan cheese on top of spinach and continue air frying for 5 minutes at 400°F until the top is nicely golden and cheese has melted.
6. Serve straight away.

Ingredients:

1/2 cup of chopped white onion.
10 oz. of frozen spinach, thawed.
1 tsp. of salt.
1 tsp. of ground black pepper.
2 tsp. of minced garlic.
1/2 tsp. of ground nutmeg.
4 oz. of cream cheese, reduced-fat, diced.
1/4 cup of shredded Parmesan cheese, reduced-fat.

Nutrition:

Calories: 273.
Carbs: 8 g.
Fat: 23 g.
Protein: 8 g.
Fiber: 2 g.

80. EGGPLANT PARMESAN

Preparation Time: 20'

Cooking Time: 15'

Serving: 4

Ingredients:

1/2 cup and 3 tbsp. almond flour, divided.
1.25-pound eggplant, ½-inch sliced.
1 tbsp. of chopped parsley.
1 tsp. of Italian seasoning.
2 tsp. of salt.
1 cup of marinara sauce.
1 egg, pastured.
1 tbsp. of water.
3 tbsp. of grated Parmesan cheese, reduced-fat.
1/4 cup of grated mozzarella cheese, reduced-fat.

Directions:

1. Slice the eggplant into ½-inch pieces, place them in a colander, sprinkle with 1 ½ tsp. salt on both sides, and let it rest for 15 minutes.
2. Meanwhile, place ½ cup flour in a bowl, add egg and water and whisk until blended.
3. Place remaining flour in a shallow dish, add remaining salt, Italian seasoning, and Parmesan cheese, and stir until mixed.
4. Switch on the Air Fryer, insert the fryer basket, grease it with olive oil, then shut with its lid, set the fryer to 360°F, and preheat for 5 minutes.
5. Meanwhile, drain the eggplant pieces, pat them dry, and then dip each slice into the egg mixture and coat with flour mixture.
6. Open the Air fryer, add coated eggplant slices in it in a single layer, close with its lid and cook for 8 minutes until nicely golden and cooked, flipping the eggplant slices halfway through the frying.
7. Then top each eggplant slice with a tbsp. of marinara sauce and some of the mozzarella cheese and continue air frying for 1 to 2 minutes or until cheese has melted.
8. When the Air Fryer beeps, open its lid, transfer eggplants onto a serving plate, and keep them warm.
9. Cook the remaining eggplant slices the same way and serve.

Nutrition:

Calories: 193.
Carbs: 27 g.
Fat: 5.5 g.
Protein: 10 g.
Fiber: 6 g.

81. CAULIFLOWER RICE

Preparation Time: 10'

Cooking Time: 27'

Serving: 3

Directions:

1. Switch on the Air Fryer, insert fryer pan, grease it with olive oil, then shut with its lid, set the fryer to 370°F, and preheat for 5 minutes.
2. Meanwhile, place tofu in a bowl, crumble it, then add remaining ingredients and stir until mixed.
3. Open the fryer, add tofu mixture in it, and spray with oil; close with its lid and cook for 10 minutes until nicely golden and crispy, stirring halfway through the frying.
4. Meanwhile, place all the ingredients for cauliflower in a bowl and toss until mixed.
5. When the Air Fryer beeps, open its lid, add cauliflower mixture, shake the pan gently to mix, and continue cooking for 12 minutes, shaking halfway through the frying.
6. Serve straight away.

Ingredients:

For the tofu:
1 cup of diced carrot.
6 oz of tofu, extra-firm, drained.
1/2 cup of diced white onion.
2 tbsp. of soy sauce.
1 tsp. of turmeric.

For the cauliflower:
1/2 cup of chopped broccoli.
3 cups of cauliflower rice.
1 tbsp. of minced garlic.
1/2 cup of frozen peas.
1 tbsp. of minced ginger.
2 tbsp. of soy sauce.
1 tbsp. of apple cider vinegar.
1 1/2 tsp. of toasted sesame oil.

Nutrition:

Calories: 258.1.
Carbs: 20.8 g.
Fat: 13 g.
Protein: 18.2 g.
Fiber: 7 g.

82. BRUSSELS SPROUTS

Preparation Time: 5'

Cooking Time: 10'

Serving: 2

Ingredients:

2 cups of Brussels sprouts.
1/4 tsp. of sea salt.
1 tbsp. of olive oil.
1 tbsp. of apple cider vinegar.

Directions:

1. Switch on the Air Fryer, insert the fryer basket, grease it with olive oil, then shut with its lid, set the fryer to 400°F, and preheat for 5 minutes.
2. Meanwhile, cut the sprouts lengthwise into ¼-inch thick pieces, put them in a bowl, add remaining ingredients and toss until well coated.
3. Open the fryer, add sprouts to it, close with its lid and cook for 10 minutes until crispy and cooked, shaking halfway through the frying.
4. When Air Fryer beeps, open its lid, transfer sprouts onto a serving plate and serve.

Nutrition:

Calories: 88.
Carbs: 11 g.
Fat: 4.4 g.
Protein: 3.9 g.
Fiber: 4 g.

83. GREEN BEANS

Preparation Time:
5'

Cooking Time:
13'

Serving:
4

Directions:

1. Switch on the Air Fryer, insert the fryer basket, grease it with olive oil, then shut with its lid, set the fryer to 400°F, and preheat for 5 minutes.
2. Meanwhile, place the beans in a bowl, spray generously with olive oil, sprinkle with garlic powder, black pepper, salt, and paprika and toss until well coated.
3. Open the fryer, add green beans to it, close with its lid and cook for 8 minutes until nicely golden and crispy, shaking halfway through the frying.
4. When Air Fryer beeps, open its lid, transfer green beans onto a serving plate and serve.

Ingredients:

1-pound of green beans.
¾ tsp. of garlic powder.
¾ tsp. of ground black pepper.
1 ¼ tsp. of salt.
½ tsp. of paprika.
Olive oil.

Nutrition:

Calories: 45.
Carbs: 7 g.
Fat: 1 g.
Protein: 2 g.
Fiber: 3 g.

84. ASPARAGUS AVOCADO SOUP

Preparation Time:
10'

Cooking Time:
20'

Serving:
4

Ingredients:

1 avocado, peeled, pitted, cubed.
12 oz. of asparagus.
½ tsp. of ground black pepper.
1 tsp. of garlic powder.
1 tsp. of sea salt.
2 tbsp. of olive oil, divided.
1/2 of a lemon, juiced.
2 cups of vegetable stock.

Directions:

1. Switch on the Air Fryer, insert the fryer basket, grease it with olive oil, then shut with its lid, set the fryer to 425°F, and preheat for 5 minutes.
2. Meanwhile, place asparagus in a shallow dish, drizzle with 1 tbsp. oil, sprinkle with garlic powder, salt, and black pepper and toss until well mixed.
3. Open the fryer, add asparagus to it, close with its lid and cook for 10 minutes until nicely golden and roasted, shaking halfway through the frying.
4. When Air Fryer beeps, open its lid and transfer asparagus to a food processor.
5. Add remaining ingredients into a food processor and pulse until well combined and smooth.
6. Tip the soup in a saucepan, pour in water if the soup is too thick and heat it over medium-low heat for 5 minutes until thoroughly heated.
7. Ladle soup into bowls and serve.

Nutrition:

Calories: 208.
Carbs: 13 g.
Fat: 16 g.
Protein: 6 g.
Fiber: 5 g.

85. FRIED PEPPERS WITH SRIRACHA MAYO

Preparation Time:
20'

Cooking Time:
10'

Serving:
2

Directions:

1. Toss the bell peppers and onions with olive oil, rosemary, basil, salt, and black pepper.
2. Place the peppers and onions on an even layer in the cooking basket. Cook at 400°F for 12 to 14 minutes.
3. Meanwhile, make the sauce by whisking the mayonnaise and Sriracha. Serve immediately.

Ingredients:

4 bell peppers, seeded and sliced (1-inch pieces).
1 onion, sliced (1-inch pieces).
1 tbsp. of olive oil.
1/2 tsp. of dried rosemary.
1/2 tsp. of dried basil.
Kosher salt, to taste.
1/4 tsp. of ground black pepper.
1/3 cup of mayonnaise.
1/3 tsp. of Sriracha.

Nutrition:

Calories: 346.
Fat: 34.1g.
Carbs: 9.5g.
Protein: 2.3g.
Sugars: 4.9g.

86. CLASSIC FRIED PICKLES

Preparation Time: 20'

Cooking Time: 10'

Serving: 2

Ingredients:

1 egg, whisked.
2 tbsp. of buttermilk.
1/2 cup of fresh breadcrumbs.
1/4 cup of Romano cheese, grated.
1/2 tsp. of onion powder.
1/2 tsp. of garlic powder.
1 ½ cups of dill pickle chips, pressed dry with kitchen towels.

Mayo sauce:
1/4 cup of mayonnaise.
1/2 tbsp. of mustard.
1/2 tsp. of molasses.
1 tbsp. of ketchup.
1/4 tsp. of ground black pepper.

Directions:

1. In a shallow bowl, whisk the egg with buttermilk.
2. In another bowl, mix the breadcrumbs, cheese, onion powder, and garlic powder.
3. Dip the pickle chips in the egg mixture, then, dredge with the breadcrumb/cheese mixture.
4. Cook in the preheated Air Fryer at 400°F for 5 minutes; shake the basket and cook for 5 minutes more.
5. Meanwhile, mix all the sauce ingredients until well combined. Serve the fried pickles with the mayo sauce for dipping.

Nutrition:

Calories: 342.
Fat: 28.5g.
Carbs: 12.5g.
Protein: 9.1g.
Sugars: 4.9g.

87. FRIED GREEN BEANS WITH PECORINO ROMANO

Preparation Time:
15'

Cooking Time:
10'

Serving:
3

Directions:

1. In a shallow bowl, whisk together the buttermilk and egg.
2. In a separate bowl, combine the cornmeal, tortilla chips, Pecorino Romano cheese, salt, black pepper, and paprika.
3. Dip the green beans in the egg mixture, then, in the cornmeal/cheese mixture. Place the green beans in the lightly greased cooking basket.
4. Cook in the preheated Air Fryer at 390°F for 4 minutes. Shake the basket and cook for a further 3 minutes.
5. Taste, adjust the seasonings and serve with the dipping sauce if desired. Bon appétit!

Ingredients:

2 tbsp. of buttermilk.
1 egg.
4 tbsp. of cornmeal.
4 tbsp. of tortilla chips, crushed.
4 tbsp. of Pecorino Romano cheese, finely grated.
Coarse salt and crushed black pepper, to taste.
1 tsp. of smoked paprika.
12 oz. of green beans, trimmed.

Nutrition:

Calories: 340.
Fat: 9.7g.
Carbs: 50.9g.
Protein: 12.8g.
Sugars: 4.7g.

88. SPICY ROASTED POTATOES

Preparation Time: 15'

Cooking Time: 10'

Serving: 2

Ingredients:

4 potatoes, peeled and cut into wedges.
2 tbsp. of olive oil.
Salt and black pepper to taste.
1 tsp. of cayenne pepper.
1/2 tsp. of ancho chili powder.

Directions:

1. Toss all the ingredients in a mixing bowl until the potatoes are well covered.
2. Transfer them to the Air Fryer basket and cook at 400°F for 6 minutes; shake the basket and cook for a further 6 minutes.
3. Serve wholehearted with your favorite sauce for dipping. Bon appétit!

Nutrition:

Calories: 299.
Fat: 13.6g.
Carbs: 40.9g.
Protein: 4.8g.
Sugars: 1.4g.

89. Spicy Glazed Carrots

Preparation Time: 20'

Cooking Time: 10'

Serving: 3

Directions:

1. Start by warming your Air Fryer to 380°F.
2. Toss all ingredients together and place them in the Air Fryer basket.
3. Cook for 15 minutes, shaking the basket halfway through the cooking time. Transfer to a serving platter and enjoy!

Ingredients:

1 pound carrots, cut into matchsticks.
2 tbsp. of peanut oil.
1 tbsp. of agave syrup.
1 jalapeño, seeded and minced.
1/4 tsp. of dill.
1/2 tsp. of basil.
Salt and white pepper to taste.

Nutrition:

Calories: 162.
Fat: 9.3g.
Carbs: 20.1g.
Protein: 1.4g.
Sugars: 12.8g.

90. EASY SWEET POTATO BAKE

Preparation Time: 35'

Cooking Time: 30'

Serving: 3

Ingredients:

1 stick butter, melted.
1 pound of sweet potatoes, mashed.
2 tbsp. of stevia.
2 eggs, beaten.
1/3 cup of coconut milk.
1/4 cup of flour.
1/2 cup of fresh breadcrumbs.

Directions:

1. Start by warming your Air Fryer to 325°F.
2. Grease a casserole dish with cooking oil.
3. In a mixing bowl, combine all ingredients, except for the breadcrumbs and 1 tbsp. of butter. Spoon the mixture into the prepared casserole dish.
4. Top with the breadcrumbs and brush the top with the remaining 1 tbsp. of butter. Bake in the preheated Air Fryer for 30 minutes. Bon appétit!

Nutrition:

Calories: 409.
Fat: 26.1g.
Carbs: 38.3g.
Protein: 7.2g.
Sugars: 10.9g.

91. AVOCADO FRIES WITH ROASTED GARLIC MAYONNAISE

Preparation Time: 50'

Cooking Time: 1 h

Serving: 4

Directions:

1. Put the garlic on a piece of aluminum foil and drizzle with cooking spray. Wrap the garlic in the foil.
2. Cook in the preheated Air Fryer at 400°F for 12 minutes. Check the garlic, open the top of the foil and continue to cook for 10 minutes more.
3. Let it rest for 10 to 15 minutes; remove the cloves by squeezing them out of the skins; mash the garlic and reserve.
4. In a shallow bowl, combine the flour, salt, and black pepper. In another shallow dish, whisk the eggs until frothy.
5. Place the crushed tortilla chips in a third shallow dish. Dredge the avocado wedges in the flour mixture, shaking off the excess. Then, dip in the egg mixture; last, dredge in crushed tortilla chips.
6. Sprinkle the avocado wedges with cooking oil on all sides.
7. Cook in the preheated Air Fryer at 395°F for approximately 8 minutes, turning them over halfway through the cooking time.
8. Meanwhile, combine the sauce ingredients with the smashed roasted garlic. To serve, divide the avocado fries between plates and top with the sauce. Enjoy!

Ingredients:

1/2 head garlic 6-7 cloves.
3/4 cup of all-purpose flour.
Salt and black pepper to taste.
2 eggs.
1 cup of tortilla chips, crushed.
3 avocados, cut into wedges.

Sauce:
1/2 cup of mayonnaise.
1 tsp. of lemon juice.
1 tsp. of mustard.

Nutrition:

Calories: 351.
Fat: 27.7g.
Carbs: 21.5g.
Protein: 6.4g.
Sugars: 1.1g.

92. ROASTED BROCCOLI WITH SESAME SEEDS

Preparation Time: 15'

Cooking Time: 10'

Serving: 2

Ingredients:

1-pound broccoli florets.
2 tbsp. of sesame oil.
1/2 tsp. of shallot powder.
1/2 tsp. of porcini powder.
1 tsp. of garlic powder.
Salt and pepper to taste.
1/2 tsp. of cumin powder.
1/4 tsp. of paprika.
2 tbsp. of sesame seeds.

Directions:

1. Start by warming the Air Fryer to 400°F.
2. Blanch the broccoli in salted boiling water until al dente, about 3 to 4 minutes. Drain well and transfer to the lightly greased Air Fryer basket.
3. Add the sesame oil, shallot powder, porcini powder, garlic powder, salt, black pepper, cumin powder, paprika, and sesame seeds.
4. Cook for 6 minutes, tossing them over halfway through the cooking time. Bon appétit!

Nutrition:

Calories: 267.
Fat: 19.5g.
Carbs: 20.2 g.
Protein: 8.9g.
Sugars: 5.2 g.

93. CORN ON THE COB WITH HERB BUTTER

Preparation Time: 15'

Cooking Time: 10'

Serving: 2

Directions:

1. Spray the corn with cooking spray. Cook at 395°F for 6 minutes, turning them over halfway through the cooking time.
2. In the meantime, mix the butter with the granulated: garlic, ginger, salt, black pepper, rosemary, and basil.
3. Spread the butter mixture all over the corn on the cob. Cook in the preheated Air Fryer for additional 2 minutes. Bon appétit!

Ingredients:

2 ears fresh corn, shucked and cut into halves.
2 tbsp. of butter, room temperature.
1 tsp. of granulated garlic.
1/2 tsp. of fresh ginger, grated.
Salt and pepper to taste.
1 tbsp. of fresh rosemary, chopped.
1 tbsp. of fresh basil, chopped.
2 tbsp. of fresh chives, roughly chopped.

Nutrition:

Calories: 239.
Fat: 13.3g.
Carbs: 30.2g.
Protein: 5.4g.
Sugars: 5.8g.

94. RAINBOW VEGETABLE FRITTERS

Preparation Time: 20'

Cooking Time: 10'

Serving: 2

Ingredients:

1 zucchini, grated and squeezed.
1 cup of corn kernels.
1/2 cup of canned green peas.
4 tbsp. of all-purpose flour.
2 tbsp. of fresh shallots, minced.
1 tsp. of fresh garlic, minced.
1 tbsp. of peanut oil.
Salt and pepper to taste.
1 tsp. of cayenne pepper.

Directions:

1. In a mixing bowl, thoroughly combine all the ingredients until everything is well combined.
2. Shape the mixture into patties. Spray the Air Fryer basket with cooking spray.
3. Cook in the preheated Air Fryer at 365°F for 6 minutes. Turn them over and cook for a further 6 minutes.
4. Serve immediately and enjoy!

Nutrition:

Calories: 215.
Fat: 8.4g.
Carbs: 31.6g.
Protein: 6g.
Sugars: 4.1g.

95. CAULIFLOWER AND GOAT CHEESE CROQUETTES

Preparation Time: 30'

Cooking Time: 26'

Serving: 2

Directions:

1. Put the cauliflower florets in a saucepan of water; bring to the boil; reduce the heat and cook for 10 minutes or until tender.
2. Mash the cauliflower using your blender; add the garlic, cheese, and spices; mix to combine well.
3. Form the cauliflower mixture into croquettes shapes.
4. Cook in the preheated Air Fryer at 375°F for 16 minutes, shaking halfway through the cooking time. Serve with the sour cream and mustard. Bon appétit!

Ingredients:

1/2 pound of cauliflower florets.
2 garlic cloves, minced.
1 cup of goat cheese, shredded.
Salt and pepper to taste.
1/2 tsp. of shallot powder.
1/4 tsp. of cumin powder.
1 cup of sour cream.
1 tsp. of Dijon mustard.

Nutrition:

Calories: 297.
Fat: 21.7g.
Carbs: 11.7g.
Protein: 15.3g.
Sugars: 2.6g.

Chapter 7
DIABETIC AIR FRYER SEAFOOD

96. CRAB CAKE

Preparation Time: 5'

Cooking Time: 15'

Serving: 2

Ingredients:

8 oz. crab meat, wild-caught.
2 tbsp. almond flour.
1/4 cup red bell pepper, cored, chopped.
2 green onions, chopped.
1 tsp. old bay seasoning.
1 tbsp. Dijon mustard.
2 tbsp. mayonnaise, reduced-fat.

Directions:

1. Switch on the air fryer, insert the fryer basket, grease it with olive oil, then shut with its lid, set the fryer at 370° F and preheat for 5 minutes.
2. Meanwhile, place all the ingredients in a bowl, stir until well combined and then shape the mixture into four patties.
3. Open the fryer, add crab patties in it, spray oil over the patties, close with its lid and cook for 10 minutes until nicely golden and crispy, flipping the patties halfway through the frying.
4. When the air fryer beeps, open its lid, transfer the crab patties onto a serving plate and serve with lemon wedges.

Nutrition:

Calories: 123.
Carbs: 5 g.
Fat: 6 g.
Protein: 12 g.
Fiber: 1 g.

97. SALMON

Preparation Time: 5'

Cooking Time: 12'

Serving: 2'

Directions:

1. Switch on the air fryer, insert the fryer basket, grease it with olive oil, then shut with its lid, set the fryer at 390° F and preheat for 5 minutes.
2. Meanwhile, rub each salmon fillet with oil and then season with black pepper, paprika, and salt.
3. Open the fryer, add seasoned salmon in it, close with its lid and cook for 7 minutes until nicely golden and cooked, flipping the fillets halfway through the frying.
4. When the air fryer beeps, open its lid, transfer salmon onto a serving plate and serve.

Ingredients:

2 salmon fillets, wild-caught, each about 1 ½ inch thick.
1 tsp. ground black pepper.
2 tsp. paprika.
1 tsp. salt.
2 tsp. olive oil.

Nutrition:

Calories: 288.
Carbs: 1.4 g.
Fat: 18.9 g.
Protein: 28.3 g.
Fiber: 0.8 g.

98. PARMESAN SHRIMP

Preparation Time: 10'

Cooking Time: 10'

Serving: 6'

Ingredients:

2 pounds jumbo shrimp, wild-caught, peeled, deveined.
2 tbsp. minced garlic.
1 tsp. onion powder.
1 tsp. basil.
1 tsp. ground black pepper.
1/2 tsp. dried oregano.
2 tbsp. olive oil.
2/3 cup grated parmesan cheese, reduced-fat.
2 tbsp. lemon juice.

Directions:

1. Switch on the air fryer, insert the fryer basket, grease it with olive oil, then shut with its lid, set the fryer at 350° F and preheat for 5 minutes.
2. Meanwhile, place cheese in a bowl, add remaining ingredients except for shrimps and lemon juice and stir until combined.
3. Add shrimps and then toss until well coated.
4. Open the fryer, add shrimps in it, spray oil over them, close with its lid and cook for 10 minutes until nicely golden and crispy, shaking halfway through the frying.
5. When the air fryer beeps, open its lid, transfer chicken onto a serving plate, drizzle with lemon juice and serve.

Nutrition:

Calories: 307.
Carbs: 12 g.
Fat: 16.4 g.
Protein: 27.6 g.
Fiber: 3 g.

99. FISH STICKS

Preparation Time: 5'

Cooking Time: 15'

Serving: 4

Directions:

1. Switch on the air fryer, insert the fryer basket, grease it with olive oil, then shut with its lid, set the fryer at 400° F and preheat for 5 minutes.
2. Meanwhile, place mayonnaise in a bowl and then whisk in water and mustard until blended.
3. Place pork rinds in a shallow dish, add Cajun seasoning, black pepper and salt and stir until mixed.
4. Cut the cod into 1 by 2 inches pieces, then dip into mayonnaise mixture and then coat with pork rind mixture.
5. Open the fryer, add fish sticks in it, spray with oil, close with its lid and cook for 10 minutes until nicely golden and crispy, flipping the sticks halfway through the frying.
6. When the air fryer beeps, open its lid, transfer fish sticks onto a serving plate and serve.

Ingredients:

1-pound cod, wild-caught.
½ tsp. ground black pepper.
3/4 tsp. Cajun seasoning.
1 tsp. salt.
1 1/2 cups pork rind.
1/4 cup mayonnaise, reduced-fat.
2 tbsp. water.
2 tbsp. Dijon mustard.

Nutrition:

Calories: 263.
Carbs: 1 g.
Fat: 16 g.
Protein: 26.4 g.
Fiber: 0.5 g.

100. SHRIMP WITH LEMON AND CHILE

Preparation Time: 5'

Cooking Time: 12'

Serving: 2

Ingredients:

1-pound shrimp, wild-caught, peeled, deveined.
1 lemon, sliced.
1 small red chili pepper, sliced.
½ tsp. ground black pepper.
1/2 tsp. garlic powder.
1 tsp. salt.
1 tbsp. olive oil.

Directions:

1. Switch on the air fryer, insert the fryer basket, grease it with olive oil, then shut with its lid, set the fryer at 400° F and preheat for 5 minutes.
2. Meanwhile, place shrimps in a bowl, add garlic, salt, black pepper, oil, and lemon slices and toss until combined.
3. Open the fryer, add shrimps and lemon in it, close with its lid and cook for 5 minutes, shaking halfway through the frying.
4. Then add chili slices, shake the basket until mixed and continue cooking for 2 minutes or until shrimps are opaque and crispy.
5. When the air fryer beeps, open its lid, transfer shrimps and lemon slices onto a serving plate and serve.

Nutrition:

Calories: 112.5.
Carbs: 1 g.
Fat: 1 g.
Protein: 20.4 g.
Fiber: 0.2 g.

101. TILAPIA

Preparation Time: 5'

Cooking Time: 12'

Serving: 2

Directions:

1. Switch on the air fryer, insert the fryer basket, grease it with olive oil, then shut with its lid, set the fryer at 400° F and preheat for 5 minutes.
2. Meanwhile, spray tilapia fillets with oil and then season with salt, lemon pepper, and old bay seasoning until evenly coated.
3. Open the fryer, add tilapia in it, close with its lid and cook for 7 minutes until nicely golden and cooked, turning the fillets halfway through the frying.
4. When the air fryer beeps, open its lid, transfer tilapia fillets onto a serving plate and serve.

Ingredients:

2 tilapia fillets, wild-caught, 1 ½ inch thick.
1 tsp. old bay seasoning.
¾ tsp. lemon-pepper seasoning.
½ tsp. salt.
Olive oil.

Nutrition:

Calories: 36.
Carbs: 0 g.
Fat: 0.75 g.
Protein: 7.4 g.
Fiber: 0 g.

102. TOMATO BASIL SCALLOPS

Preparation Time: 5'

Cooking Time: 15'

Serving: 2

Ingredients:

8 jumbo sea scallops, wild-caught.
1 tbsp. tomato paste.
12 oz. frozen spinach, thawed and drained.
1 tbsp. chopped fresh basil.
1 tsp. ground black pepper.
1 tsp. minced garlic.
1 tsp. salt.
3/4 cup heavy whipping cream, reduced-fat.

Directions:

1. Switch on the air fryer, insert the fryer basket, grease it with olive oil, then shut with its lid, set the fryer at 350° F and preheat for 5 minutes.
2. Meanwhile, take a 7 inches baking pan, grease it with oil and place spinach in it in an even layer.
3. Spray the scallops with oil, sprinkle with ½ tsp. each of salt and black pepper and then place scallops over the spinach.
4. Place tomato paste in a bowl, whisk in cream, basil, garlic, and remaining salt and black pepper until smooth, and then pour over the scallops.
5. Open the fryer, place the pan in it, close with its lid and cook for 10 minutes until thoroughly cooked and sauce is hot.
6. Serve straight away.

Nutrition:

Calories: 359.
Carbs: 6 g.
Fat: 33 g.
Protein: 9 g.
Fiber: 1 g.

103. SHRIMP SCAMPI

Preparation Time: 5'

Cooking Time: 12'

Serving: 4

Directions:

1. Switch on the air fryer, insert fryer pan, grease it with olive oil, then shut with its lid, set the fryer at 330° F and preheat for 5 minutes.
2. Add butter in it along with red pepper and garlic and cook for 2 minutes or until the butter has melted.
3. Then add remaining ingredients in the pan, stir until mixed and continue cooking for 5 minutes until shrimps have cooked, stirring halfway through.
4. When done, remove the pan from the air fryer, stir the shrimp scampi, let it rest for 1 minute and then stir again.
5. Garnish shrimps with basil leaves and serve.

Ingredients:

1-pound shrimp, peeled, deveined.
1 tbsp. minced garlic.
1 tbsp. minced basil.
1 tbsp. lemon juice.
1 tsp. dried chives.
1 tsp. dried basil.
2 tsp. red pepper flakes.
4 tbsp. butter, unsalted.
2 tbsp. chicken stock.

Nutrition:

Calories: 221.
Carbs: 1 g.
Fat: 13 g.
Protein: 23 g.
Fiber: 0 g.

104. SALMON CAKES

Preparation Time: 5'

Cooking Time: 12'

Serving: 2

Ingredients:

½ cup almond flour.
15 oz. cooked pink salmon.
¼ tsp. ground black pepper.
2 tsp. Dijon mustard.
2 tbsp. chopped fresh dill.
2 tbsp. mayonnaise, reduced-fat.
1 egg, pastured.
2 wedges of lemon.

Directions:

1. Switch on the air fryer, insert the fryer basket, grease it with olive oil, then shut with its lid, set the fryer at 400° F and preheat for 5 minutes.
2. Meanwhile, place all the ingredients in a bowl, except for lemon wedges, stir until combined and then shape into four patties, each about 4-inches.
3. Open the fryer, add salmon patties in it, spray oil over them, close with its lid and cook for 12 minutes until nicely golden and crispy, flipping the patties halfway through the frying.
4. When the air fryer beeps, open its lid, transfer salmon patties onto a serving plate and serve.

Nutrition:

Calories: 517.
Carbs: 15 g.
Fat: 27 g.
Protein: 52 g.
Fiber: 5 g.

105. CILANTRO LIME SHRIMPS

Preparation Time: 25'

Cooking Time: 21'

Serving: 4

Directions:

1. Take 6 wooden skewers and let them soak in warm water for 20 minutes.
2. Meanwhile, switch on the air fryer, insert the fryer basket, grease it with olive oil, then shut with its lid, set the fryer at 350° F and let preheat.
3. Whisk together lemon juice, paprika, salt, cumin, and garlic in a large bowl, then add shrimps and toss until well coated.
4. Drain the skewers and then thread shrimps in them.
5. Open the fryer, add shrimps in it in a single layer, spray oil over them, close with its lid and cook for 8 minutes until nicely golden and cooked, turning the skewers halfway through the frying.
6. When the air fryer beeps, open its lid, transfer shrimps onto a serving plate and keep them warm.
7. Cook remaining shrimp skewers in the same manner and serve.

Ingredients:

1/2-pound shrimp, peeled, deveined.
1/2 tsp. minced garlic.
1 tbsp. chopped cilantro.
1/2 tsp. paprika.
¾ tsp. salt.
1/2 tsp. ground cumin.
2 tbsp. lemon juice.

Nutrition:

Calories: 59.
Carbs: 0.3 g.
Fat: 1.5 g.
Protein: 11 g.
Fiber: 0 g.

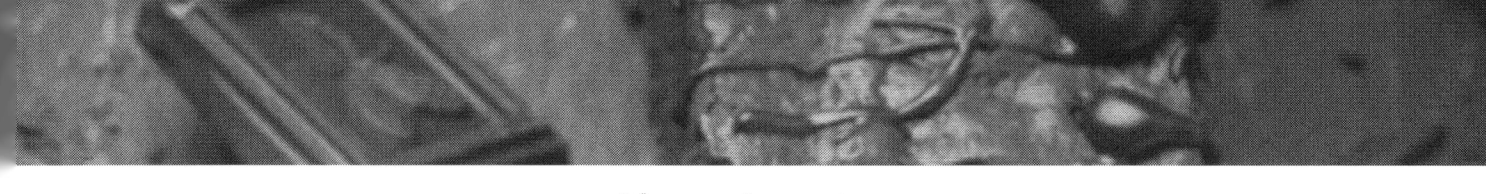

Chapter 8
DIABETIC AIR FRYER DESSERTS

106. PANCAKES

Preparation Time: 5'

Cooking Time: 29'

Serving: 4

Ingredients:

1 1/2 cup of coconut flour.
1 tsp. of salt.
3 1/2 tsp. of baking powder.
1 tbsp. of Erythritol sweetener.
1 1/2 tsp. of baking soda.
3 tbsp. of melted butter.
1 1/4 cups of milk, unsweetened, reduced-fat.
1 egg, pastured.

Directions:

1. Switch on the Air Fryer, insert fryer pan, grease it with olive oil, then shut with its lid, set the fryer to 220°F, and preheat for 5 minutes.
2. Meanwhile, take a medium bowl, add all the ingredients in it, whisk until well blended and then let the mixture rest for 5 minutes.
3. Open the fryer, pour in some of the pancake mixture as thin as possible, close with its lid and cook for 6 minutes until nicely golden, turning the pancake halfway through the frying.
4. When Air Fryer beeps, open its lid, transfer pancake onto a serving plate and use the remaining batter for cooking more pancakes the same way.
5. Serve straight away with fresh fruit slices.

Nutrition:

Calories: 237.7.
Carbs: 39.2 g.
Fat: 10.2 g.
Protein: 6.3 g.
Fiber: 1.3 g.

107. ZUCCHINI BREAD

Preparation Time: 25'

Cooking Time: 40'

Serving: 8

Directions:

1. Switch on the Air Fryer, insert the fryer basket, grease it with olive oil, then shut with its lid, set the fryer to 310°F, and preheat for 10 minutes.
2. Meanwhile, place flour in a bowl, add salt, cocoa powder, and baking soda and stir until mixed.
3. Crack the eggs in another bowl, whisk in sweetener, egg, oil, butter, and vanilla until smooth and then slowly whisk in flour mixture until well combined.
4. Add zucchini along with 1/3 cup chocolate chips and then fold until just mixed.
5. Take a mini loaf pan that fits into the Air Fryer, grease it with olive oil, then pour in the prepared batter and sprinkle remaining chocolate chips on top.
6. Open the fryer, place the loaf pan in it, close with its lid and cook for 30 minutes at the 310°F until inserted toothpick into the bread slides comes out clean.
7. When Air Fryer beeps, open its lid, remove the loaf pan, then place it on a wire rack and let the bread cool in it for 20 minutes.
8. Take out the bread, let it cool completely, then cut it into slices and serve.

Ingredients:

¾ cup of shredded zucchini.
1/2 cup of almond flour.
1/4 tsp. of salt.
1/4 cup of cocoa powder, unsweetened.
1/2 cup of chocolate chips, unsweetened, divided.
6 tbsp. of Erythritol sweetener.
1/2 tsp. of baking soda.
2 tbsp. of olive oil.
1/2 tsp. of vanilla extract, unsweetened.
2 tbsp. of butter, unsalted, melted.
1 egg, pastured.

Nutrition:

Calories: 356.
Carbs: 49 g.
Fat: 17 g.
Protein: 5.1 g.
Fiber: 2.5 g.

108. BLUEBERRY MUFFINS

Preparation Time: 10'

Cooking Time: 30'

Serving: 14

Ingredients:

1 cup of almond flour.
1 cup of frozen blueberries.
2 tsp. of baking powder.
1/3 cup of Erythritol sweetener.
1 tsp. of vanilla extract, unsweetened.
½ tsp. of salt.
¼ cup of melted coconut oil.
1 egg, pastured.
¼ cup of applesauce, unsweetened.
¼ cup of almond milk, unsweetened.

Directions:

1. Switch on the Air Fryer, insert the fryer basket, grease it with olive oil, then shut with its lid, set the fryer at 360°F, and preheat for 10 minutes.
2. Meanwhile, place flour in a large bowl, add blueberries, salt, sweetener, baking powder, and stir until well combined.
3. Crack the eggs in another bowl, whisk in vanilla, milk, and applesauce until combined, and then slowly whisk in flour mixture until well combined.
4. Take fourteen silicone muffin cups, grease them with oil, and then evenly fill them with the prepared batter.
5. Open the fryer; stack muffin cups in it, close with its lid and cook for 10 minutes until muffins are nicely golden brown and set.
6. When the Air Fryer beeps, open its lid, transfer muffins onto a serving plate, and then remaining muffins in the same manner.
7. Serve straight away.

Nutrition:

Calories: 201.
Carbs: 27.3 g.
Fat: 8.8 g.
Protein: 3 g.
Fiber: 1.2 g.

109. BAKED EGGS

Preparation Time: 5'

Cooking Time: 17'

Serving: 2

Directions:

1. Switch on the Air Fryer, insert the fryer basket, grease it with olive oil, then shut with its lid, set the fryer at 330°F, and preheat for 5 minutes.
2. Meanwhile, take two silicon muffin cups, grease them with oil, then crack an egg into each cup and evenly add cheese, spinach, and milk.
3. Season the egg with salt and black pepper and gently stir the ingredients without breaking the egg yolk.
4. Open the fryer, add muffin cups to it, close with its lid and cook for 8 to 12 minutes until eggs have cooked to desired doneness.
5. When the Air Fryer beeps, open its lid, take out the muffin cups and serve.

Ingredients:

2 tbsp. of frozen spinach, thawed.
½ tsp. of salt.
¼ tsp. of ground black pepper.
2 eggs, pastured.
3 tsp. of grated Parmesan cheese, reduced-fat.
2 tbsp. of milk, unsweetened, reduced-fat.

Nutrition:

Calories: 161.
Carbs: 3 g.
Fat: 11.4 g.
Protein: 12.1 g.
Fiber: 1.1 g.

110. BAGELS

Preparation Time:	Cooking Time:	Serving:
10'	20'	6

Ingredients:

2 cups of almond flour.
2 cups of shredded mozzarella cheese, low-fat.
2 tbsp. of butter, unsalted.
1 1/2 tsp. of baking powder.
1 tsp. of apple cider vinegar.
1 egg, pastured.

For egg wash:
1 egg, pastured.
1 tsp. butter, unsalted, melted.

Directions:

1. Place flour in a heatproof bowl, add cheese and butter, then stir well and microwave for 90 seconds until butter and cheese have melted.
2. Then stir the mixture until well combined, let it cool for 5 minutes and whisk in the egg, baking powder, and vinegar until well combined and the dough comes together.
3. Let the dough cool for 10 minutes, then divide the dough into six sections, shape each section into a bagel and let the bagels rest for 5 minutes.
4. Prepare the egg wash and for this, place the melted butter in a bowl, whisk in the egg until blended, and then brush the mixture generously on top of each bagel.
5. Take a fryer basket, line it with parchment paper, and then place prepared bagels in it in a single layer.
6. Switch on the Air Fryer, insert fryer, then shut with its lid, set the fryer to 350°F, and cook for 10 minutes at 350°F until bagels are nicely golden and thoroughly cooked, turning the bagels halfway through the frying.
7. When the Air Fryer beeps, open its lid, transfer bagels to a serving plate, and cook the remaining bagels the same way.
8. Serve straight away.

Nutrition:

Calories: 408.7.
Carbs: 8.3 g.
Fat: 33.5 g.
Protein: 20.3 g.
Fiber: 4 g.

111. CAULIFLOWER HASH BROWNS

Preparation Time:
10'

Cooking Time:
25'

Serving:
6

Directions:

1. Switch on the Air Fryer, insert the fryer basket, grease it with olive oil, then shut with its lid, set the fryer to 375°F, and preheat for 10 minutes.
2. Meanwhile, place all the ingredients in a bowl, stir until well mixed and then shape the mixture into six rectangular disks, each about ½-inch thick.
3. Open the fryer, add hash browns in it in a single layer, close with its lid and cook for 25 minutes at 375°F until nicely golden and crispy, turning halfway through the frying.
4. When the Air Fryer beeps, open its lid, transfer hash browns to a serving plate and serve.

Ingredients:

1/4 cup of chickpea flour.
4 cups of cauliflower rice.
1/2 medium white onion, peeled and chopped.
1/2 tsp. of garlic powder.
1 tbsp. of xanthan gum.
1/2 tsp. of salt.
1 tbsp. of nutritional yeast flakes.
1 tsp. of ground paprika.

Nutrition:

Calories: 115.2.
Carbs: 6.2 g.
Fat: 7.3 g.
Protein: 7.4 g.
Fiber: 2.2 g.

112. CHICKEN SANDWICH

Preparation Time: 40'

Cooking Time: 20'

Serving: 6

Ingredients:

4 chicken breasts, pastured.
1 cup of almond flour.
¾ tsp. of ground black pepper.
1/2 tsp. of paprika.
1 tsp. of salt.
1/2 tsp. of celery seeds.
1 tsp. of potato starch.
1/4 cup of milk, reduced-fat.
4 cups of dill pickle juice as needed.
2 eggs, pastured.
4 hamburger buns.
1/8 tsp. of dry milk powder, nonfat.
¼ tsp. of xanthan gum.
1/8 tsp. of Erythritol sweetener.

Directions:

1. Place the chicken in a large plastic bag, seal the bag and then pound the chicken with a mallet until ½-inch thick.
2. Brine the chicken and for this, pour the dill, pickle juice in the plastic bag containing chicken, then seal it and let the chicken soak for a minimum of 2 hours.
3. After 2 hours, remove the chicken from the brine, rinse it well, and pat dry with paper towels.
4. Place flour in a shallow dish, add black pepper, paprika, salt, celery, potato starch, milk powder, xanthan gum, sweetener, and stir until well mixed.
5. Crack eggs in another dish and then whisk until blended.
6. Switch on the Air Fryer, insert the fryer basket, grease it with olive oil, then shut with its lid, set the fryer to 375°F, and preheat for 5 minutes.
7. Meanwhile, dip the chicken into the egg and then coat it evenly with the flour mixture.
8. Open the fryer, add chicken breasts to it in a single layer, close with its lid, then cook for 10 minutes, flip the chickens and continue cooking for 5 minutes or until chicken is nicely golden and cooked.
9. When the Air Fryer beeps, open its lid, transfer chicken to a plate, and cook the remaining chicken the same way.
10. Sandwich a chicken breast between toasted hamburger buns, top with favorite dressing, and serve.

Nutrition:

Calories: 440.
Carbs: 40 g.
Fat: 19 g.
Protein: 28 g.
Fiber: 12 g.

113. TOFU SCRAMBLE

Preparation Time: 5'

Cooking Time: 18'

Serving: 3

Directions:

1. Switch on the Air Fryer, insert the fryer basket, grease it with olive oil, then shut with its lid, set the fryer at 220°F, and preheat for 5 minutes.
2. Meanwhile, place tofu pieces in a bowl, drizzle with oil, and sprinkle with xanthan gum and toss until well coated.
3. Add remaining ingredients to the tofu and then toss until well coated.
4. Open the fryer, add tofu to it, close with its lid and cook for 13 minutes until nicely golden and crispy, shaking the basket every 5 minutes.
5. When the Air Fryer beeps, open its lid, transfer tofu onto a serving plate and serve.

Ingredients:

12 oz. of tofu, extra-firm, drained, ½-inch cubed.
1 tsp. of garlic powder.
1 tsp. of onion powder.
1 tsp. of paprika.
1/2 tsp. of ground black pepper.
1/2 tsp. of salt.
1 tbsp. of olive oil.
2 tsp. of xanthan gum.

Nutrition:

Calories: 94.
Carbs: 5 g.
Fat: 5 g.
Protein: 6 g.
Fiber: 0 g.

114. FRIED EGG

Preparation Time: 5'

Cooking Time: 4'

Serving: 1

Ingredients:

1 egg, pastured.
1/8 tsp. of salt.
1/8 tsp. of cracked black pepper.
Olive oil.

Directions:

1. Take the fryer pan, grease it with olive oil and then crack the egg in it.
2. Switch on the Air Fryer, insert fryer pan, then shut with its lid, and set the fryer to 370°F.
3. Set the frying time to 3 minutes, then when the Air Fryer beep, open its lid and check the egg; if the egg needs more cooking, then Air Fryer it for another minute.
4. Transfer the egg to a serving plate, season with salt and black pepper, and serve.

Nutrition:

Calories: 90.
Carbs: 0.6 g.
Fat: 7 g.
Protein: 6.3 g.
Fiber: 0 g.

115. CHEESECAKE BITES

Preparation Time:
40'

Cooking Time:
9'

Serving:
4

Directions:

1. Prepare the cheesecake mixture, and for this, place softened cream cheese in a bowl, add cream, vanilla, and ½-cup of sweetener and whisk using an electric mixer until smooth.
2. Scoop the mixture on a baking sheet lined with a parchment sheet, then place it in the freezer for 30 minutes until firm.
3. Place flour in a small bowl and stir in the remaining sweetener.
4. Then switch on the Air Fryer, insert the fryer basket, grease it with olive oil, then shut with its lid, set the fryer at 350°F, and preheat for 5 minutes.
5. Meanwhile, cut the cheesecake mix into bite-size pieces and then coat it with an almond flour mixture.
6. Open the fryer, add cheesecake bites in it, close with its lid and cook for 2 minutes until nicely golden and crispy.
7. Serve straight away.

Ingredients:

1/2 cup of almond flour.
1/2 cup of and 2 tbsp. Erythritol sweetener, divided.
8 oz. of cream cheese, reduced-fat, softened.
1/2 tsp. of vanilla extract, unsweetened.
4 tbsp. of heavy cream, reduced-fat, divided.

Nutrition:

Calories: 198.
Carbs: 6 g.
Fat: 18 g.
Protein: 3 g.
Fiber: 0 g.

116. COCONUT PIE

Preparation Time: 5'

Cooking Time: 45'

Serving: 6

Ingredients:

1/2 cup of coconut flour.
1/2 cup of Erythritol sweetener.
1 cup of shredded coconut, unsweetened, divided.
1/4 cup of butter, unsalted.
1 1/2 tsp. of vanilla extract, unsweetened.
2 eggs, pastured.
1 1/2 cups of milk, low-fat, unsweetened.
¼ cup of shredded coconut, toasted.

Directions:

1. Switch on the Air Fryer, insert the fryer basket, grease it with olive oil, then shut with its lid, set the fryer to 350°F, and preheat for 5 minutes.
2. Meanwhile, place all the ingredients in a bowl and whisk until well blended and smooth batter comes together.
3. Take a 6-inches pie pan, grease it with oil, then pour in the prepared batter and smooth the top.
4. Open the fryer, place the pie pan in it, close with its lid, and cook for 45 minutes until pie has set and when inserted a toothpick into the pie, it slides out clean.
5. When the Air Fryer beeps, open its lid, take out the pie pan and let it cool.
6. Garnish the pie with toasted coconut, then cut into slices and serve.

Nutrition:

Calories: 236.
Carbs: 16 g.
Fat: 16 g.
Protein: 3 g.
Fiber: 2 g.

117. CRUSTLESS CHEESECAKE

Preparation Time: 5'

Cooking Time: 10'

Serving: 2

Directions:

1. Switch on the Air Fryer, insert the fryer basket, grease it with olive oil, then shut with its lid, set the fryer to 350°F, and preheat for 5 minutes.
2. Meanwhile, take two 4 inches of springform pans, grease them with oil, and set them aside.
3. Crack the eggs in a bowl and then whisk in lemon juice, sweetener and vanilla until smooth.
4. Whisk in cream cheese and sour cream until blended, and then divide the mixture evenly between prepared pans.
5. Open the fryer, place pans in it, close with its lid, and cook for 10 minutes until cakes are set and an inserted skewer into the cakes slides out clean.
6. When the Air Fryer beeps, open its lid. Please take out the cake pans and let the cakes cool in them.
7. Take out the cakes, refrigerate for 3 hours until cooled, and then serve.

Ingredients:

16 oz. of cream cheese, reduced-fat, softened.
2 tbsp. of sour cream, reduced-fat.
3/4 cup of Erythritol sweetener.
1 tbsp. of vanilla extract, unsweetened.
2 eggs, pastured.
1/2 tsp. of lemon juice.

Nutrition:

Calories: 318.
Carbs: 1 g.
Fat: 29.7 g.
Protein: 11.7 g.
Fiber: 0 g.

118. CHOCOLATE CAKE

Preparation Time: 5'

Cooking Time: 15'

Serving: 6

Ingredients:

1/4 cup of coconut flour.
1 tsp. of baking powder.
1/3 cup of Truvia sweetener.
1/4 tsp. of salt.
2 tbsp. of cocoa powder, unsweetened.
1 tsp. of vanilla extract, unsweetened.
4 tbsp. of butter, unsalted, melted.
3 eggs, pastured.
1/2 cup of heavy whipping cream, reduced-fat.

Directions:

1. Switch on the Air Fryer, insert the fryer basket, grease it with olive oil, then shut with its lid, set the fryer to 350°F, and preheat for 5 minutes.
2. Meanwhile, take a 6 cups muffin pan, grease it with oil, and set aside until required.
3. Place melted butter in a bowl, whisk in sweetener until blended, and then beat in vanilla, eggs, and cream until combined.
4. Add remaining ingredients, beat again until well combined and smooth batter comes together, and then pour the mixture into the prepared pan.
5. Open the fryer, place the pan in it, close with its lid and cook for 10 minutes until the cake is done and an inserted skewer into the cake slides out clean.
6. When the Air Fryer beeps, open its lid, take out the cake pan and let the cake cool in it.
7. Please, take out the cakes, cut them into pieces, and serve.

Nutrition:

Calories: 192.
Carbs: 8 g.
Fat: 16 g.
Protein: 4 g.
Fiber: 2 g.

119. CHOCOLATE BROWNIES

Preparation Time: 10'

Cooking Time: 45'

Serving: 4

Directions:

1. Switch on the Air Fryer, insert the fryer basket, grease it with olive oil, then shut with its lid, set the fryer to 350°F, and preheat for 10 minutes.
2. Meanwhile, place chocolate chips and butter in a heatproof bowl and microwave for 1 minute or until chocolate has melted, stirring every 30 seconds.
3. Crack eggs in another bowl, beat in vanilla and sweetener until smooth, and then slowly beat in melted chocolate mixture until well combined.
4. Take a spring-form pan that fist into the Air Fryer, grease it with oil, and then pour in batter in it.
5. Open the fryer, place the pan in it, close with its lid, and cook for 35 minutes until the cake is done and an inserted toothpick into the brownies slides out clean.
6. When the Air Fryer beeps, open its lid. Please take out the pan and let the brownies cool in it.
7. Then take out the brownies, cut them into even pieces, and serve.

Ingredients:

1/2 cup of chocolate chips.
1 tsp. of vanilla extract, unsweetened.
1/4 cup of Erythritol sweetener.
1/2 cup of butter, unsalted.
3 eggs, pastured.

Nutrition:

Calories: 224.
Carbs: 3 g.
Fat: 23 g.
Protein: 4 g.
Fiber: 1 g.

120. SPICED APPLES

Preparation Time: 5'

Cooking Time: 17'

Serving: 4

Ingredients:

4 small apples, cored, sliced.
2 tbsp. of Erythritol sweetener.
1 tsp. of apple pie spice.
2 tbsp. of olive oil.

Directions:

1. Switch on the Air Fryer, insert the fryer basket, grease it with olive oil, then shut with its lid, set the fryer to 350°F, and preheat for 5 minutes.
2. Meanwhile, place apple slice in a bowl, sprinkle with sweetener and spice, and drizzle with oil and stir until evenly coated.
3. Open the Fryer, add apple slices to it, close with its lid and cook for 12 minutes until nicely golden and crispy, shaking halfway through the frying.
4. Serve straight away.

Nutrition:

Calories: 89.6.
Carbs: 21.8 g.
Fat: 2 g.
Protein: 0.5 g.
Fiber: 5.3 g.

121. PUMPKIN CUSTARD

Preparation Time: 2 h 30'

Cooking Time: 0

Serving: 6

Directions:

1. Grease or spray a slow cooker with butter or coconut oil spray.
2. In a medium mixing bowl, beat the eggs until smooth. Then add in the sweetener.
3. To the egg mixture, add in the pumpkin puree along with vanilla or maple extract.
4. Then add almond flour to the mixture along with the pumpkin pie spice and salt. Add melted butter, coconut oil, or ghee.
5. Transfer the mixture into a slow cooker. Close the lid. Cook for 2-2 ¾ hours on Low.
6. When through, serve with whipped cream, and then sprinkle with little nutmeg if needed. Enjoy!
7. Set slow-cooker to the Low setting. Cook for 2-2.45 hours, and begin checking at the two-hour mark. Serve warm with stevia-sweetened whipped cream and a sprinkle of nutmeg.

Ingredients:

1/2 cup of almond flour.
4 eggs.
1 cup of pumpkin puree.
1/2 cup of stevia/erythritol blend, granulated.
1/8 tsp. of sea salt.
1 tsp. of vanilla extract or maple flavoring.
4 tbsp. of butter, ghee, or coconut oil melted.
1 tsp. of pumpkin pie spice.

Nutrition:

Calories: 70.
Total fat: 0.7g.
Saturated fat: 0.1g.
Total carbs: 14.7g.
Net carbs: 12.2g.
Protein: 2.1g.
Sugar: 2.2g.
Fiber: 2.5g.
Sodium: 1mg.

122. PEANUT BUTTER BANANA "ICE CREAM"

Preparation Time: 10'

Cooking Time: 0'

Serving: 6

Ingredients:

4 medium bananas.
½ cup of whipped peanut butter.
1tsp. of vanilla extract.

Directions:

1. Peel the bananas and slice them into coins.
2. Arrange the slices on a plate and freeze until solid.
3. Place the frozen bananas in a food processor.
4. Add the peanut butter and mix until it is mostly smooth.
5. Scrape down the sides, then add the vanilla extract.
6. Mix until smooth, then spoon into bowls to serve.

Nutrition:

Calories: 70.
Total fat: 0.7g.
Saturated fat: 0.1g.
Total carbs: 14.7g.
Net carbs: 12.2g.
Protein: 2.1g.
Sugar: 2.2g.
Fiber: 2.5g.
Sodium: 1mg.

123. FRUITY COCONUT ENERGY BALLS

Preparation Time:
15'

Cooking Time:
0'

Serving:
18

Directions:

1. Put the almonds, figs, apricots, and cranberries in a food processor.
2. Blend the mixture until finely chopped.
3. Add the vanilla extract and cinnamon, then blend to combine once more.
4. Roll the mixture into 18 small balls by hand.
5. Roll the balls in the shredded coconut and chill until firm.

Ingredients:

1 cup of chopped almonds.
1 cup of dried figs.
½ cup of dried apricots, chopped.
½ cup of dried cranberries, unsweetened.
½ tsp. of vanilla extract.
¼ tsp. of ground cinnamon.
½ cup of shredded unsweetened coconut.

Nutrition:

Calories: 100.
Total fat: 0.7g.
Saturated fat: 0.1g.
Total carbs: 14.7g.
Net carbs: 12.2g.
Protein: 2.1g.
Sugar: 2.2g.
Fiber: 2.5g.
Sodium: 1mg.

124. Mini Apple Oat Muffins

Preparation Time: 5'

Cooking Time: 25'

Serving: 24

Ingredients:

1 ½ cups of old-fashioned oats.
1 tsp. of baking powder.
½ tsp. of ground cinnamon.
¼ tsp. of baking soda.
¼ tsp. of salt.
½ cup of unsweetened applesauce.
¼ cup of light.
3 tbsp. of canola oil.
3 tbsp. of water.
1 tsp. of vanilla extract.
½ cup of slivered almonds.

Directions:

1. Preheat the oven to 350°F and grease a mini muffin pan.
2. Place the oats in a food processor and mix them into a fine flour.
3. Add the baking powder, cinnamon, baking soda, and salt.
4. Mix until well combined, add the applesauce, canola oil, water, and vanilla and then blend smooth.
5. Fold in the almonds and spoon the mixture into the muffin pan.
6. Bake for 22 to 25 minutes until a knife inserted in the center comes out clean.
7. Cool the muffins for 5 minutes, then turn them out onto a wire rack.

Nutrition:

Calories: 70.
Total fat: 0.7g.
Saturated fat: 0.1g.
Total carbs: 14.7g.
Net carbs: 12.2g.
Protein: 2.1g.
Sugar: 2.2g.
Fiber: 2.5g.
Sodium: 1mg.

125. DARK CHOCOLATE ALMOND YOGURT CUPS

Preparation Time: 10'

Cooking Time: 0'

Serving: 6

Directions:

1. Whisk together the yogurt, almond extract, and liquid stevia in a medium bowl.
2. Spoon the yogurt into four dessert cups.
3. Sprinkle with chopped chocolate and slivered almonds.

Ingredients:

3 cups of plain nonfat Greek yogurt.
½ tsp. of almond extract.
¼ tsp. of liquid stevia extract (more to taste).
2 oz. 70% dark chocolate, chopped.
½ cup of slivered almonds.

Nutrition:

Calories: 170.
Total fat: 0.7g.
Saturated fat: 0.1g.
Total carbs: 14.7g.
Net carbs: 12.2g.
Protein: 2.1g.
Sugar: 2.2g.
Fiber: 2.5g.
Sodium: 41mg.

126. CHOCOLATE AVOCADO MOUSSE

Preparation Time: 5'

Cooking Time: 0'

Serving: 3

Ingredients:

1 large avocado, pitted and chopped.
¼ cup of fat-free milk.
¼ cup of unsweetened cocoa powder (dark).
2 tsp. of powdered stevia.
1 tsp. of vanilla extract.
2 tbsp. of fat-free whipped topping.

Directions:

1. Place the avocado in a food processor and blend smoothly.
2. In a small bowl, whisk together the milk and cocoa powder until well mixed.
3. Stir in the pureed avocado along with the stevia and vanilla extract.
4. Spoon into bowls and serve with fat-free whipped topping.

Nutrition:

Calories: 180.
Total fat: 0.7g.
Saturated fat: 0.1g.
Total carbs: 14.7g.
Net carbs: 12.2g.
Protein: 2.1g.
Sugar: 2.2g.
Fiber: 2.5g.
Sodium: 23mg.

Melissa Simson

127. PUMPKIN SPICE SNACK BALLS

Preparation Time:
15'

Cooking Time:
10'

Serving:
10

Directions:

1. Preheat the oven to 300°F and line a baking sheet with parchment.
2. Combine the oats, almonds, and coconut on the baking sheet.
3. Bake for 8 to 10 minutes until browned, stirring halfway through.
4. Place the pumpkin, stevia, pumpkin pie spice, and salt in a medium bowl.
5. Stir in the toasted oat mixture.
6. Shape the mixture into 20 balls by hand and place on a tray.
7. Chill until the balls are firm, then serve.

Ingredients:

1 ½ cups of old-fashioned oats.
½ cup of chopped almonds.
½ cup of unsweetened shredded coconut.
¾ cup of canned pumpkin puree.
2 tbsp. of stevia.
2 tsp. of pumpkin pie spice.
¼ tsp. of salt.

Nutrition:

Calories: 170.
Total fat: 0.7g.
Saturated fat: 0.1g.
Total carbs: 14.7g.
Net carbs: 12.2g.
Protein: 2.1g.
Sugar: 2.2g.
Fiber: 2.5g.
Sodium: 1mg.

128. STRAWBERRY LIME PUDDING

Preparation Time: 15'

Cooking Time: 10'

Serving: 4

Ingredients:

2 cups plus 2 tbsp. fat-free milk.
2 tsp. of flavorless gelatin.
10 large strawberries, sliced.
1 tbsp. of fresh lime zest.
2 tsp. of vanilla extract.
Liquid stevia extract, to taste.

Directions:

1. Whisk together 2 tbsp. of milk and gelatin in a medium bowl until the gelatin dissolves completely.
2. Place the strawberries in a food processor with lime juice and vanilla extract.
3. Blend until smooth, then pour into a medium bowl.
4. Warm the remaining milk in a small saucepan over medium heat.
5. Stir in the lime zest and heat until steaming (do not boil).
6. Gently whisk the gelatin mixture into the hot milk, then stir in the strawberry mixture.
7. Sweeten with liquid stevia to taste and chill until set. Serve cold.

Nutrition:

Calories: 70.
Total fat: 0.7g.
Saturated fat: 0.1g.
Total carbs: 14.7g.
Net carbs: 12.2g.
Protein: 2.1g.
Sugar: 2.2g.
Fiber: 2.5g.
Sodium: 1mg.

129. Cinnamon Toasted Almonds

Preparation Time: 5'

Cooking Time: 25'

Serving: 8

Directions:

1. Preheat the oven to 325°F and line a baking sheet with parchment.
2. Toss together the almonds, olive oil, cinnamon, and salt.
3. Spread the almonds on the baking sheet in a single layer.
4. Bake for 25 minutes, stirring several times until toasted.

Ingredients:

2 cups of whole almonds.
1 tbsp. of olive oil.
1 tsp. of ground cinnamon.
½ tsp. of salt.

Nutrition:

Calories: 150.
Total fat: 13.6g.
Saturated fat: 1.2g.
Total carbs: 5.3g.
Net carbs: 2.2g.
Protein: 5g.
Sugar: 1g.
Fiber: 3.1g.
Sodium: 148mg.

130. GRAIN-FREE BERRY COBBLER

Preparation Time: 5'

Cooking Time: 25'

Serving: 10

Ingredients:

4 cups of fresh mixed berries.
½ cup of ground flaxseed.
¼ cup of almond meal.
¼ cup of unsweetened shredded coconut.
½ tbsp. of baking powder.
1 tsp. of ground cinnamon.
¼ tsp. of salt.
Powdered stevia, to taste.
6 tbsp. of coconut oil.

Directions:

1. Preheat the oven to 375°F and lightly grease a 10-inch cast-iron skillet.
2. Spread the berries on the bottom of the skillet.
3. Whisk together the dry ingredients in a mixing bowl.
4. Cut in the coconut oil using a fork to create a crumbled mixture.
5. Spread the crumble over the berries and bake for 25 minutes until hot and bubbling.
6. Cool the cobbler for 5 to 10 minutes before serving.

Nutrition:

Calories: 215.
Total fat: 13.6g.
Saturated fat: 1.2g.
Total carbs: 5.3g.
Net carbs: 2.2g.
Protein: 5g.
Sugar: 1g.
Fiber: 3.1g.
Sodium: 67mg.

131. WHOLE-WHEAT PUMPKIN MUFFINS

Preparation Time:
15'

Cooking Time:
15'

Serving:
36

Directions:

1. Preheat the oven to 350°F and grease two 24-cup mini muffin pans with cooking spray.
2. Whisk together the flour, baking powder, baking soda, cinnamon, pumpkin pie spice, and salt in a large mixing bowl.
3. In a separate bowl, whisk together the eggs, pumpkin, applesauce, vanilla extract, and milk.
4. Stir the wet ingredients into the dry ones until well blended.
5. Adjust sweetness to taste with liquid stevia extract, if desired.
6. Spoon the batter into 36 cups and bake for 12 to 15 minutes until cooked through.

Ingredients:

1 ¾-cup of whole-wheat flour.
1 tsp. of baking powder.
1 tsp. of baking soda.
1 tsp. of ground cinnamon.
1 tsp. of pumpkin pie spice.
½ tsp. of salt.
2 large eggs.
1 cup of canned pumpkin puree.
1/3 cup of unsweetened applesauce.
¼ cup of light.
1 tsp. of vanilla extract.
1/3 cup of fat-free milk.
Liquid stevia extract, to taste.

Nutrition:

Calories: 35.
Total fat: 13.6g.
Saturated fat: 1.2g.
Total carbs: 5.3g.
Net carbs: 2.2g.
Protein: 5g.
Sugar: 1g.
Fiber: 3.1g.
Sodium: 53mg.

132. HOMEMADE MUFFINS

Preparation Time: 10'

Cooking Time: 15'

Serving: 3

Ingredients:

6 tbsp. of olive oil.
2 eggs.
100g of flour.
1 tsp. of Royal baking powder.
Lemon zest.

Directions:

1. Beat the eggs, with the help of a whisk. Add the oil little by little while stirring until you get a fluffy cream. Then add the lemon zest.
2. Finally, add the sifted flour with the yeast to the previous mixture and mix in an envelope.
3. Fill 2/3 of the muffin baking tray with the dough.
4. Preheat the Air Fryer a few minutes to 180°C, and when ready, place the muffins in the basket.
5. Set the timer for approximately 20 minutes at a temperature of 180°C, until they are golden brown.

Nutrition:

Calories: 240.
Fat: 12g.
Carbs: 29 g.
Protein: 4g.
Sugar: 100g.
Cholesterol: 67g.

133. CHOCOLATE AND NUT CAKE

Preparation Time:
10'

Cooking Time:
30'

Serving:
4

Directions:

1. Melt the dark chocolate with the butter over low heat. Once melted, put in a bowl.
2. Mix the egg, flour, yeast (the latter passed through the sieve to prevent lumps from forming), and finally, the chopped nuts.
3. Beat well by hand until you get a uniform dough.
4. Put the dough in a silicone mold or oven suitable for incorporation in the Air Fryer's basket.
5. Preheat the Air Fryer a few minutes at 180ºC.
6. Set the timer for 20 minutes at 180ºC, and when it has cooled down, unmold.

Ingredients:

60g of dark chocolate.
2 butter spoons.
1 egg.
50g flour.
1 envelope of Royal yeast.
Chopped walnuts.

Nutrition:

Calories: 108.
Fat: 12g.
Carbs: 29g.
Protein: 4g.
Sugar: 100g.
Cholesterol: 3g.

134. STEVIA WALNUT ROASTED PEARS

Preparation Time: 7'

Cooking Time: 18-23'

Serving: 4

Ingredients:

2 large Bosc pears, halved and seeded.
3 tbsp. stevia.
1 tbsp. unsalted butter.
½ tsp. ground cinnamon.
¼ cup chopped walnuts.
¼ cup part-skim low-fat ricotta cheese, divided.

Directions:

1. In a baking pan, place the pears cut side up.
2. In a small microwave-safe bowl, melt the stevia, butter, and cinnamon. Brush this mixture over the cut sides of the pears.
3. Pour 3 tbsp. of water around the pears in the pan. Roast at 350°F (177°C) for 18 to 23 minutes, or until tender when pierced with a fork and slightly crisp on the edges, basting once with the liquid in the pan.
4. Carefully remove the pears from the pan and place them on a serving plate. Drizzle each with some liquid from the pan, sprinkle the walnuts on top, and serve with a spoonful of ricotta cheese.

Nutrition:

Calories: 139.
Fat: 4 g.
Protein: 2 g.
Carbs: 25 g.
Fiber: 3 g.
Sugar: 21 g.
Sodium: 17 mg.

135. ALMOND PEARS

Preparation Time: 10'

Cooking Time: 15-20'

Serving: 4

Directions:

1. Stir almond flavoring into yogurt and set aside while preparing pears.
2. Halve each pear and spoon out the core.
3. Place pear halves in the air fryer basket.
4. Stir together the cookie crumbs and almonds. Place a quarter of this mixture into the hollow of each pear half.
5. Cut butter into 4 pieces and place one piece on top of the crumb mixture in each pear.
6. Roast at 360°F (182°C) for 15 to 20 minutes or until pears have cooked through but are still slightly firm.
7. Serve pears warm with a dollop of yogurt topping.

Ingredients:

¼ tsp. almond flavoring.
1 container vanilla Greek yogurt (5 to 6 oz. / 142 to 170 g).
2 whole pears.
¼ cup crushed Biscoff cookies (about 4 cookies).
1 tbsp. sliced almonds.
1 tbsp. butter.

Nutrition:

Calories: 116.
Fat: 4 g.
Protein: 5 g.
Carbs: 15 g.
Fiber: 3 g.
Sugar: 10 g.
Sodium: 19 mg.

Chapter 9
30 DAY MEAL PLAN

Day	Breakfast	Lunch	Dinner	Desserts
1	Asparagus cheese strata	Mustard-crusted sole	Roasted vegetable and chicken salad	Pancakes
2	Vegetable frittata	Almond crusted cod with chips	Chicken satay	Zucchini bread
3	Egg and avocado breakfast burrito	Stevia lemon snapper with fruit	Chicken fajitas with avocados	Blueberry muffins
4	Mixed berry Dutch pancake	Easy tuna wraps	Crispy buttermilk fried chicken	Baked eggs
5	Crunchy fried French toast sticks	Asian-inspired swordfish steaks	Garlicky chicken with creamer potatoes	Cauliflower hash browns
6	Pumpkin oatmeal with raisins	Salmon with fennel and carrot	Baked chicken cordon bleu	Chicken sandwich
7	Mushroom and black bean burrito	Ranch tilapia fillets	Chicken tenders and vegetables	Tofu scramble
8	Bacon and egg sandwiches	Chilean sea bass with green olive relish	Greek chicken kebabs	Fried egg
9	Stuffed bell peppers	Ginger and green onion fish	Tandoori chicken	Cheesecake bites
10	Almond crunch granola	Asian sesame cod	Stevia lemon garlic chicken	Coconut pie

11	Yogurt raspberry cake	Roasted shrimp and veggies	Baked lemon pepper chicken drumsticks	Crustless cheesecake
12	Spinach and tomato egg cup	Lemon scallops with asparagus	Balsamic glazed chicken	Chocolate cake
13	Egg muffins with bell pepper	Fish tacos	Harissa roasted Cornish game hens	Chocolate brownies
14	Egg-in-a-hole	Spicy Cajun shrimp	Stevia mustard turkey breast	Spiced apples
15	Egg and cheese pockets	Garlic parmesan roasted shrimp	South Indian pepper chicken	Pumpkin custard
16	Huevos rancheros	Quick shrimp scampi	Mini turkey meatloaves	Peanut butter banana "ice cream"
17	Jalapeño potato hash	Pork spare ribs	Roasted vegetable and chicken salad	Fruity coconut energy balls
18	Asparagus cheese strata	BBQ pork ribs	Chicken satay	Mini apple oat muffins
19	Vegetable frittata	Mustard-crusted sole	Chicken fajitas with avocados	Dark chocolate almond yogurt cups
20	Egg and avocado breakfast burrito	Almond crusted cod with chips	Crispy buttermilk fried chicken	Chocolate avocado mousse
21	Mixed berry Dutch pancake	Stevia lemon snapper with fruit	Garlicky chicken with creamer potatoes	Pumpkin spice snack balls
22	Crunchy fried French toast	Easy tuna wraps	Baked chicken cordon bleu	Strawberry lime pudding

		sticks			
23	Pumpkin oatmeal with raisins	Asian-inspired swordfish steaks	Chicken tenders and vegetables	Cinnamon toasted almonds
24	Mushroom and black bean burrito	Salmon with fennel and carrot	Greek chicken kebabs	Grain-free berry cobbler
25	Bacon and egg sandwiches	Ranch tilapia fillets	Tandoori chicken	Whole-wheat pumpkin muffins
26	Stuffed bell peppers	Chilean sea bass with green olive relish	Stevia lemon garlic chicken	Homemade muffins
27	Almond crunch granola	Ginger and green onion fish	Baked lemon pepper chicken drumsticks	Chocolate and nut cake
28	Yogurt raspberry cake	Asian sesame cod	Balsamic glazed chicken	Stevia walnut roasted pears
29	Spinach and tomato egg cup	Roasted shrimp and veggies	Harissa roasted Cornish game hens	Almond pears
30	Egg muffins with bell pepper	Lemon scallops with asparagus	Stevia mustard turkey breast	Pancakes

CONCLUSION

Using an Air Fryer can be hard at first. If you follow our tips and tricks in this book, you will cook like a pro in no time! We have listed all sorts of recipes in this book so that you can make sure that you never run out of gas while trying to make your favorite foods again! Make sure to read through the whole book so that you can get everything right.

There's something about Air-fryers. When you think about it, they're kind of like a meal in a bit, without the hassle of actually cooking. All you have to do is grab a slice of bread or your favorite dish (or even a sandwich!), place it in the appliance, and wait for it to cook.

Air-fryers are convenient because they can be used at all hours. You can use them for cooking your favorite dish for dinner while you're getting ready or just for a quick snack in the middle of the day. You can even use them for cooking large meals such as breakfast foods or ethnic dishes overnight and saving yourself from having to clean up after dinner.

When you're using an Air-fryer, though, be careful about what foods you use. Some foods are difficult or impossible to fry when using an Air-fryer, so avoid using certain ingredients such as breaded chicken and pancakes with syrup or butter. There may be some other things you want to avoid, too, so be sure to check out our article on the diabetic Air-fryer cookbook.

The Diabetic Air-Fryer Cookbook provides a complete guide to using your air-fryer for the first time. In this section, you will learn everything you need to know about using your Air-fryer. It covers some basic information as well as advanced techniques.

This cookbook is designed to teach you some of the basics about how to use your Air-fryer, allowing you to enjoy all of its great features. We start with a shortlist of rules and tips that will help you make sure you are using your Air-fryer correctly. We also provide links in this section so that you can learn later if needed.

Diabetic Air Fryer Cookbook

In Diabetic Air-Fryer Cookbook, we provide a full selection of accessories to help you use your Air-fryer more effectively. We provide an extensive selection of tools to repair your Air-fryer and make sure it is in a peak condition and lasts as long as possible.

After reading our cookbook, you'll find that we've covered all of the bases when it comes to using your Air Fryer. You'll be able to cook healthy food every time with little effort and save money in the process! Make healthier choices without sacrifice from using this innovative and easy-to-use appliance!

This book will help you master the art of air frying and make your favorite meals completely pain-free and healthier than ever. One of the best ways to cook healthy food in a microwave is to use the air frying method. It involves cooking with steam, without oil or fats. This means that your kitchen will be free from a "fried" smell, and you can have a healthier diet.

This cookbook's contents will help you learn exactly how to do this by following step-by-step instructions that will be written for you without confusing words or often-used terms. We will teach you how to prepare and cook delicious and nutritious dishes quickly and easily when cooked using an Air Fryer. You can make breakfast, lunch, dinner, snacks, and desserts, so easily using this method. You will be able to prepare them in under 30 minutes without storing or freezing the ingredients because the foods are not fried at all.

It is just one of the key things that you can get from this book. Along with the "how-to" instructions, you will also receive helpful tips and tricks to help you when cooking with an Air Fryer.

Printed in Great Britain
by Amazon